Contents

Introduction			4
Training and Exam practice			
Test 1	Paper 1	Reading	10
	Paper 2	Writing	20
	Paper 3	Use of English	35
	Paper 4	Listening	49
	Paper 5	Speaking	58
Test 2	Paper 1	Reading	67
	Paper 2	Writing	73
	Paper 3	Use of English	86
	Paper 4	Listening	94
	Paper 5	Speaking	100
Practice Tests			
Test 3	Paper 1	Reading	108
	Paper 2	Writing	114
	Paper 3	Use of English	116
	Paper 4	Listening	121
	Paper 5	Speaking	125
Test 4	Paper 1	Reading	127
	Paper 2	Writing	133
	Paper 3	Use of English	135
	Paper 4	Listening	140
	Paper 5	Speaking	144
Test 5	Paper 1	Reading	146
	Paper 2	Writing	152
	Paper 3	Use of English	154
	Paper 4	Listening	159
	Paper 5	Speaking	163
Test 6	Paper 1	Reading	165
	Paper 2	Writing	171
	Paper 3	Use of English	173
	Paper 4	Listening	178
	Paper 5	Speaking	182
Answer sheets			184
Acknowledgements			189
Speaking appendix	*(colour section pages C1–C24)*		

Introduction

Who is *First Certificate Trainer* for?

This book is suitable for anyone who is preparing to take the Cambridge First Certificate in English (FCE). You can use *First Certificate Trainer* in class with your teacher, or – in the case of the with-answers edition of the book – on your own at home.

What is *First Certificate Trainer*?

First Certificate Trainer contains six practice tests for FCE, each covering the Reading, Writing, Use of English, Listening and Speaking papers. Guided Tests 1 and 2 consist of both training and practice for the exam, while Tests 3–6 are entirely practice. All six tests are at exam level and are of FCE standard.

Test 1 contains information about each part of each paper, plus step-by-step guidance to take you through each kind of FCE task type, with examples and tips clearly linked to the questions. In the Writing, Use of English and Speaking papers, it also presents and practises grammar, vocabulary and functional language directly relevant to particular task types. This is supported by work on correcting common grammar mistakes made by FCE candidates in the exam as shown by the **Cambridge Learner Corpus**. For more information on the Cambridge Learner Corpus see page 6. In Writing, you work with extracts from actual candidate scripts from the Corpus, and in Speaking you listen to sample recordings of each part of the paper. The Explanatory answer key tells you which answers are correct and why, and explains why other possible answers are wrong.

Test 2 also contains training for the exam, in addition to revision from Test 1. Here too there is language input, as well as some step-by-step guidance to task types with further examples, advice and tips. In Writing there is a full focus on the task types not covered in Test 1.

Tests 3–6 contain a wide range of topics, text types and exam items, enabling you to practise the skills you have developed and the language you have learnt in Tests 1 and 2.

How to use *First Certificate Trainer*

Test 1 Training

- For each part of each paper you should begin by studying **Task information**, which tells you the facts you need to know, such as what the task type tests and the kinds of questions it uses.
- Throughout Test 1, you will see information marked **Tip!** These tips give you practical advice on how to tackle each task type.
- In all papers, training exercises help you develop the skills you need, e.g. reading for gist, by working through example items of a particular task type.
- Answers to all the training exercises are in the **Explanatory answer key** of the with-answers edition.
- For every part of Writing, Use of English and Speaking, **Useful language** presents and practises grammatical structures, vocabulary or functional expressions that are often tested by particular task types.
- Many exercises involve focusing on and correcting common language mistakes made by actual First Certificate candidates, as shown by the **Cambridge Learner Corpus** (see page 6).

••• Peter May

First Certificate TRAINER

SIX PRACTICE TESTS
WITHOUT ANSWERS

CAMBRIDGE UNIVERSITY PRESS
Cambridge, New York, Melbourne, Madrid, Cape Town, Singapore,
São Paulo, Delhi, Dubai, Tokyo, Mexico City

Cambridge University Press
The Edinburgh Building, Cambridge CB2 8RU, UK

www.cambridge.org
Information on this title: www.cambridge.org/9780521139274

© Cambridge University Press 2010

This publication is in copyright. Subject to statutory exception
and to the provisions of relevant collective licensing agreements,
no reproduction of any part may take place without the written
permission of Cambridge University Press.

First published 2010

Printed in the United Kingdom at the University Press, Cambridge

A catalogue record for this publication is available from the British Library

ISBN 978-0-521-13547-4 Audio CDs
ISBN 978-0-521-13927-4 Practice Tests
ISBN 978-0-521-12853-7 Practice Tests with Answers and Audio CDs

Cambridge University Press has no responsibility for the persistence or
accuracy of URLs for external or third-party internet websites referred to in
this publication, and does not guarantee that any content on such websites is,
or will remain, accurate or appropriate. Information regarding prices, travel
timetables and other factual information given in this work are correct at
the time of first printing but Cambridge University Press does not guarantee
the accuracy of such information thereafter.

- In **Listening**, you are prompted to use one of the numbered **CDs**, e.g. CD1 01. If you are working on your own using the with-answers edition of *First Certificate Trainer*, you will need a CD player (or a computer that plays CDs) plus a watch or clock to make sure you keep to the times allowed for each part of the test.
- In **Writing**, Test 1 covers Part 1, as well as the letter, essay and article tasks in Part 2. You study **sample answers** from the **Cambridge Learner Corpus** written by actual First Certificate candidates in the exam, as well as model answers to help you perfect your skills. The Explanatory answer key contains answers to the exercises, plus more model texts. You finish each part by writing your own text, bringing in what you have learnt in **Useful language**.
- In **Speaking**, you are prompted to use one of the numbered CDs, e.g. CD2 01, and do written tasks while you listen to examples of each part of the paper. You can practise speaking on your own or with a partner, using what you have learnt in **Useful language**.
- In all papers, **Action plan** gives you clear step-by-step guidance on how to approach each task type.
- You then work through an FCE-style task, often doing exercises based on the guidance in **Action plan** and then following the exam instructions. As you do so, **Advice** boxes suggest ways of dealing with particular exam items.
- Answers to all items are in the **Explanatory answer key**, which explains why the correct answers are right and others are wrong. For Listening, the parts of the **transcripts** which give the correct answers are underlined in the texts.

Test 2 Training
- Test 2 contains many of the same features as Test 1, including exercises that focus on exam instructions, texts and tasks, **Tip!** information, **Advice** boxes for many exam items, **Useful language** and an **Explanatory answer key**.
- There is further work based on mistakes frequently made by First Certificate candidates as shown by the **Cambridge Learner Corpus**.
- There is also an emphasis on revision, with cross-references for each task type to the relevant **Task information** and **Action plan** in Test 1. You should refer back to these before you begin working through each part.
- Test 2 **Writing** covers Part 1 plus the report, review, short story and set text tasks in Part 2, also with sample answers and authentic candidates' texts from the **Cambridge Learner Corpus**.
- You should try to do the exam tasks under exam conditions where possible.

Tests 3–6 Exam practice
- In Tests 3, 4, 5 and 6, you can apply the skills and language you have learnt in Guided Tests 1 and 2.
- You can do these tests and the 5 papers within them in any order, but you should always try to keep to the time recommended for each paper. For the Listening paper, you must **listen to each recording twice only**.
- It will be easier to keep to the exam instructions if you can find somewhere quiet to work, and ensure there are no interruptions.
- For the Speaking paper it is better if you can work with a partner, but if not, you can follow the instructions and do all four parts on your own.
- If you have the with-answers edition of the book, you can check your answers for yourself, and also study the Listening transcripts after you have completed the tasks.

Introduction | 5

The Cambridge Learner Corpus (CLC)

The Cambridge Learner Corpus (CLC) is a large collection of exam scripts written by candidates taking Cambridge ESOL English exams around the world. It currently contains over 85,000 scripts and is growing all the time. It forms part of the Cambridge International Corpus (CIC) and it has been built up by Cambridge University Press and Cambridge ESOL. The CLC currently contains scripts from over:

- 85,000 students
- 100 different first languages
- 180 different countries

Exercises and extracts from candidates' answers from Writing in *First Certificate Trainer* which are based on the CLC are indicated by this icon: ◉ Find out about the Cambridge Learner Corpus at www.cambridge.org/corpus.

Other features of *First Certificate Trainer*

- Full-colour **visual material** for the Speaking paper of all six tests in the Speaking appendix.
- For Tests 1 and 2, the **Explanatory answer key** in the with-answers edition on pages 184–234 tells you which answers are correct, and why. In some cases, such as multiple-choice questions, it also explains why the other possible answers are wrong.
- In the **with-answers** edition, you can check you answers to Tests 3–6 in the key at the back. In the case of Listening, the parts of the transcript that give the correct answers are underlined.
- **Photocopiable answer sheets** for the Reading, Use of English and Listening papers are at the back of the book. Before you take the exam, you should study these so that you know how to mark or write your answers correctly. In Writing, the question paper has plenty of lined space for you to write your answers.
- **3 audio CDs** containing recordings for the Listening papers of the six First Certificate tests plus recordings of different parts of the Speaking test to serve as samples. The listening material is indicated by a different icon in *First Certificate Trainer* for each of the CDs:
  🎧01 🎧01 🎧01

The Cambridge First Certificate in English examination

Level of the First Certificate in English examination

First Certificate is at level B2 on the Common European Framework (CEF). When you reach this level, these are some of the things you should be able to do:

- You can scan written texts for the information you need, and understand detailed instructions or advice.
- You can understand or give a talk on a familiar subject, and keep a conversation going on quite a wide range of subjects.
- You can make notes while someone is talking, and write a letter that includes different kinds of requests.

Grading

- The overall First Certificate grade that you receive is based on the total score you achieve in all five papers.

- Each paper – Reading, Writing, Use of English, Listening and Speaking – has a maximum possible weighted score of 40 marks.
- There is no minimum score for each paper, so you don't have to 'pass' all five in order to pass the exam.
- You receive a certificate if you pass the exam with grade A (the highest grade), B or C. Grades D and E are fails.
- Whatever your grade, you will receive a Statement of Results. This includes a graphical profile of how well you did in each paper and shows your relative performance in each one.
- For more information on grading and results, go to the Cambridge ESOL website (see 'Further information' on page 9).

Content of the First Certificate in English examination

The Cambridge First Certificate in English examination has five papers, each consisting of 2, 3 or 4 parts. For details on each part, see the page reference under the *Task information* heading in these tables.

Paper 1 Reading 1 hour

Texts are usually of about 550–700 words each, making an overall total of around 2,000 words. They are taken from newspaper and magazine articles, fiction, report, advertisements, correspondence, messages and informational material such as brochures, guides or manuals. There are 2 marks for each correct answer in Parts 1 and 2; there is 1 mark for every right answer in Part 3.

Part	Task type	No. of questions	Format	Task information
1	multiple choice	8	You read a text followed by questions with four options: A, B, C or D.	page 10
2	gapped text	7	You read a text with sentences removed, then fill in the gaps by choosing sentences from a jumbled list.	page 14
3	multiple matching	15	You read one or more texts and match the relevant sections to what the questions say.	page 17

Paper 2 Writing 1 hour 20 minutes

You have to do Part 1 (question 1) plus any **one** of the Part 2 tasks. In Part 2 you can choose one of questions 2–4 or else either of the two options in question 5. The possible marks for Part 1 and Part 2 are the same. In all tasks you are told who you are writing to, and why.

Part	Task type	No. of words	Format	Task information
1	letter or email	120–150	You write in response to an input text of up to 160 words.	page 20
2	Questions 2–4 possible tasks: letter, essay, article, report, review or story	120–180	You do a task based on a situation.	pages 24, 28, 32, 76, 79, 82
	Question 5 possible tasks: article, essay, letter, report, or review	120–180	You do a task based on one of two set reading texts.	page 85

Introduction | 7

Paper 3 Use of English 45 minutes

Parts 1 and 3 mainly test your vocabulary; Part 2 mainly tests your grammar. Part 4 often tests both. There is one mark for each correct answer in Parts 1, 2 and 3, but often two marks for a right answer in Part 4. You can write on the question paper, but you must remember to transfer your answers to the separate answer sheet before the end of the test.

Part	Task type	No. of questions	Format	Task information
1	multiple choice gap-fill	12	You choose from words A, B, C or D to fill in each gap in a text.	page 35
2	open gap-fill	12	You think of a word to fill in each of the gaps in a text.	page 39
3	word formation	10	You think of the right form of a given word to fill in each gap in a text.	page 42
4	key word transformations	8	You have to complete a sentence with a given word so that it means the same as another sentence.	page 45

Paper 4 Listening about 40 minutes

You will both hear and see the instructions for each task, and you will hear each of the four parts twice. You will hear pauses announced, and you can use this time to look at the task and the questions. At the end of the test you will have five minutes to copy your answers onto the answer sheet.

If one person is speaking, you may hear information, news, instructions, a commentary, a documentary, a lecture, a message, a public announcement, a report, a speech, a talk or an advertisement. If two people are talking, you might hear a conversation, a discussion, an interview, part of a radio play, etc.

Part	Task type	No. of questions	Format	Task information
1	multiple choice	8	You hear one or two people talking for about 30 seconds in eight different situations. For each question, you choose from answers A, B or C.	page 49
2	sentence completion	10	You hear one or two people talking for about three minutes. For each question, you complete sentences by writing a word or short phrase.	page 52
3	multiple matching	5	You hear five different extracts, of about 30 seconds each, with a common theme. For each one you choose from a list of six possible answers.	page 54
4	multiple choice	7	You hear one or two people talking for about three minutes. For each question, you choose from answers A, B or C.	page 56

Paper 5 Speaking 14 minutes

You will probably do the Speaking test with one other candidate, though sometimes it is necessary to form groups of three. There will be two examiners, but one of them does not take part in the conversation. The examiner will indicate who you should talk to in each part of the test.

Part	Task type	Minutes	Format	Task information
1	The examiner asks you some questions.	3–4	You talk about yourself.	page 58
2	You talk on your own.	3–4	You talk about two pictures and then comment on the other candidate's pictures.	page 60
3	You talk to the other candidate.	3–4	You discuss some diagrams or pictures together.	page 63
4	You talk about things connected with the topic of Part 3.	3–4	You take part in a discussion with both the other candidate and the examiner.	page 65

Further information

The information about FCE contained in *First Certificate Trainer* is designed to be an overview of the exam. For a full description of the First Certificate in English examination, including information about task types, testing focus and preparation for the exam, please see the *FCE Handbook*, which can be obtained from Cambridge ESOL at the address below or from the website at: www.CambridgeESOL.org.

University of Cambridge ESOL Examinations
1 Hills Road
Cambridge CB1 2EU
United Kingdom

Test 1 Training — PAPER 1 Reading Part 1

Task information

- In part 1 you read a text followed by eight questions with four options: **A**, **B**, **C** or **D**.
- Questions may test your ability to understand overall meaning, main ideas or details, as well as attitudes or opinions.
- You may need to *infer* meaning (use clues to understand things that aren't actually said).
- The first line can be a question or an unfinished statement.
- Questions follow the order of information in the text, but question 8 may test your overall understanding.

Reading for gist; dealing with distraction

1 Quickly read the exam instructions and the two paragraphs.

1 What kind of text is it?
2 Why did Liam go to the house?

You are going to read an extract from a novel. For questions **1–8**, choose the answer (**A**, **B**, **C** or **D**) which you think fits best according to the text.

It was late afternoon when Liam stepped off the train and made his way quickly out of Upton station. As ever in autumn it was damp, cold and windy, with low clouds racing across the darkening sky. He thought about taking a bus into town, but remembered how infrequent they were and decided to go on foot instead. There was hardly anyone around, though at a street corner he passed four teenagers he recognised. 'Hi,' he said, but there was no reply and he hurried on. Further along the road a young couple he was sure he knew passed by on the other side, but when he gave them a wave they just looked the other way. 'This used to be my home town,' Liam said to himself, 'but it doesn't feel like it any more.'

Arriving at number 46, he rang the bell and waited. At first nobody came, even though he was right on time and he knew that Carson was expecting him. He rang again, more impatiently. He didn't want to be there a moment longer than necessary. He wondered whether Carson might have changed his mind about helping. Had the plan perhaps become so ambitious that it had scared him off? Eventually, though, the door opened, and a tall, thin, worried-looking man stood there. 'Did you have a good journey? Is everything all right?' Carson asked. 'Yes,' said Liam calmly, 'and if you can give me the package, I'll be on my way.'

2 Look at exam question 1 below: the answer is C. The parts of the text that relate to options A–D are underlined. Write A, B, C or D next to the underlined text and explain why each option is right or wrong.

1 What surprised him about the town?

    A   There were many people on the streets.
    B   The public transport system was poor.
    Ⓒ   The people he saw were unfriendly.
    D   The weather was rather unpleasant.

3 Look at exam question 2 below: the answer is B. Underline the parts of the text that relate to options A–D and explain why each is right or wrong.

2 How did Liam feel when he was at the house?

    A   pleased he would be able to spend some time there
    Ⓑ   eager to collect the item and then leave quickly
    C   afraid because he was involved in something big
    D   worried that he might have got there too late

 Tip! Look for clear evidence that the answer you have chosen is right, and that the other three are wrong.

Test 1 Exam practice — Reading Part 1

Action plan

1 Read the instructions and the title, if there is one. What kind of text (e.g. *magazine article*) is it?

2 Quickly read the text without trying to answer any of the questions. What is it about?

Tip! You don't need to understand every word of the text to be able to answer the questions, so don't spend too much time on expressions you don't know.

3 Look at the stem of the first question, underlining the key words.

4 Find the relevant part of the text and draw a vertical line next to it, writing down the question number.

5 Read what the text says about the question and try to answer in your own words.

6 Look at options A, B, C and D. Which is closest to your understanding of what the text says?

Tip! Choose your answer according to **what the text says**, not what you think the right answer should be from your general knowledge, or your own opinions.

7 If you really aren't sure, cross out any options that are definitely wrong then make a guess.

8 Repeat steps 1–7 for each question.

Follow the exam instructions on page 12, using the advice on page 13 to help you.

Tip! Questions may ask you to work out the meaning of words or phrases using the context, or focus on reference words like *it* and *this*.

Tip! Questions could be about the use of examples or comparison, the writer's purpose, or the tone, e.g. *critical*, of the text.

You are going to read part of an article about an Arctic explorer. For questions **1–8**, choose the answer (**A**, **B**, **C** or **D**) which you think fits best according to the text.

Alone to the North Pole

Photographer Christina Franco wants to become the first woman to reach the geographic North Pole solo and on foot. She tells Emma Smith about it.

Sixty days walking over ice and snow in temperatures as low as –45°C, with nothing to keep you company except the occasional polar bear. This is no small achievement. Only a few people have ever walked to the North Pole unassisted, and if Christina Franco succeeds, she will have earned a place in the history books and met one of the few remaining challenges of exploration left to women.

Her 480-mile journey will begin in northern Canada, dragging a sledge that weighs as much as she does. At the end of each day's walking or skiing, she will pitch her tent in sub-zero temperatures, get into a sleeping bag filled with ice, and attempt to sleep to the unsettling background sounds of howling wind and cracking ice, which may or may not signal the approach of one of those polar bears. 'I'll carry a pistol to scare any bears away,' says Franco, 42. 'The bears that far north won't have had contact with humans, fortunately, so they won't associate me with food, but they will be curious and that's dangerous. If it uses a paw to see what you are, it could damage your tent – or your arm. I imagine I'll have quite a few sleepless nights.'

Many of the early polar explorers suffered from disease and injuries, and while modern technology (lightweight materials, satellite phones, planes on stand-by to carry out rescue missions) has lessened the dangers, it can never make such an inhospitable landscape anything approaching safe. It can take just five minutes for any uncovered skin to become frostbitten and, once the sun has risen, Franco will only be able to remove her sunglasses inside her tent, otherwise the intensity of the sunlight reflecting off the snow would cause snow blindness. Just to heighten the danger, the cold will slow down her brain functions, so it will be more difficult to make split-second decisions in the event of a sudden crisis.

She will use about 8,000 calories a day, losing nearly half a kilogram every 24 hours. 'The problem is the human body can only take on about 5,500 calories a day,' she says. 'So you have to fatten up before you set off or you'll run out of energy.' Franco is currently trying to put on 19 kilos. She may complain about not fitting into any of her dresses, but when Franco weighs herself in front of me and finds she's lost one kilo rather than gained two, as she'd expected, she's very upset. 'I hope my scales are wrong because, if not, I've lost weight,' she says, reaching for one of many bars of chocolate lying around her kitchen.

Born in Italy, Franco moved to New York and then to London. She has become well known locally, thanks to a training routine that involves dragging a tractor tyre around the streets, fastened by a rope around her waist. When I meet her she is about to head out along the canal near her home. 'I get a lot of comments,' she says, laughing. 'Cars stop and people take pictures. They think it's really funny. Occasionally people sit on it when I'm not looking, or pull on it, to make it more difficult.'

Franco, who hopes her walk will raise money to fund research into motor neurone disease, has long been fascinated by exploring. 'I remember, as a child, learning about the Italian Arctic explorer Umberto Nobile,' she explains. 'There are certain things that catch your imagination. The idea of people getting into frozen sleeping bags. It was remarkable to me, the idea of pushing the body like that and you didn't just die. These things get hold of you and, if one day the opportunity comes your way, you can't help yourself. Now, when I think how horrible it's going to be, I know I've only got myself to blame!'

And if she gets there, will she celebrate? 'Yes, my mum's going to come in the plane to pick me up. She's very worried and she hates the cold, but she's going to conquer her fears to come and celebrate with me . . . if I make it.'

1 What does the writer say about the history of exploration?
   A Walking to the North Pole used to be considered easier than other journeys.
   B No woman has ever completed the journey to the geographic North Pole.
   C Female explorers have already done most of the world's difficult journeys.
   D Christina is already an important historical figure for her previous journeys.

2 'Unsettling' (line 12) means
   A comforting.
   B worrying.
   C exciting
   D surprising.

3 What does Christina say about the danger from polar bears?
   A They could injure her without meaning to.
   B If they are hungry, they might attack her.
   C In that part of the Arctic they are harmless.
   D She will have to shoot any that attack her.

4 Which of these is a real risk to Christina during her walk?
   A She won't be able to think very quickly in emergencies.
   B Sunlight reflected by the snow could quickly burn her skin.
   C She will need to protect her eyes, even during the night.
   D If she's ill or has an accident, there will be no medical care.

5 Why, when she is talking to the writer, does Christina want to eat chocolate?
   A She feels that she has little energy at the moment.
   B She's just found out her weight has gone down.
   C She knows that her weight is actually going up.
   D She always eats chocolate when she's upset.

6 Some people are amused when they
   A realise that she trains next to a canal.
   B hear the funny remarks she often makes.
   C learn that she intends to walk to the North Pole.
   D see her pulling a heavy object behind her.

7 She decided to walk to the North Pole when she
   A managed to survive a night in freezing conditions.
   B was at last able to do something she felt she had to do.
   C realised she was ill and she needed to pay for treatment.
   D first heard about a famous explorer from her country.

8 What impression do we get of Christina's attitude towards the walk?
   A She now regrets deciding to go.
   B She wants to do it, but not alone.
   C She knows how tough it will be.
   D She's sure she will reach the Pole.

Advice

1 The questions are in the same order as the information in the text, so which part of the text is likely to mention this?

2 How often do these sounds occur? Will she be pleased to hear them? Why?/Why not?

3 Read carefully to find out how bears might be a danger to humans.

4 Look for a word that means 'risks' and the examples of this.

5 What happened before she went to take the chocolate?

6 Decide what the pronoun 'it' means in the last two sentences of the paragraph.

7 What was her reaction when she had the chance to do the walk?

8 Look at her comments at various points in the text, but particularly near the end.

Reading Part 1   Test 1 Exam practice | 13

Test 1 Training — Reading Part 2

Task information

- In Part 2, there is a text with seven gaps (9–15). Each gap is for a missing sentence. These sentences are in a list (A–H), but in the wrong order. You have to put the sentences into the right gaps.
- There is also a sentence that doesn't fit anywhere. This can be any of A–H.
- You can use each sentence A–H once only.
- Part 2 tests your understanding of the overall structure of the text, and the development of ideas, opinions and events.
- The instructions tell you what kind of text it is and what it is about.
- The text has a title, and often some background information below it.

Predicting text content; finding clues

1 Read the title and the sentence below it in *italics*. What do you think the text will be about?

2 Study the extract. Gap 9 has the correct answer (F) and the expressions which link sentence F to the text are underlined. Match each link in sentence F and an underlined part of the text, e.g. *biologists/the scientists*.

The flight of the bee

New research explains the mystery of why bees never seem to get lost.

Those who have studied bees have long wondered how they always manage to find their way home. No matter how strong the cross-winds, they never seem to get blown off course. Now, however, <u>biologists</u> believe they have discovered their secret – by using radar to <u>observe their flight patterns</u>. **9** **F** To do <u>so</u>, they fitted bees with tiny electronic instruments, which enabled <u>the scientists</u> to <u>track all their movements over several kilometres</u>. What <u>this</u> showed <u>them</u> was that bees seem to know exactly how far the wind is blowing them off course, and they react to this by adjusting their flight direction accordingly.

Aircraft pilots do something similar, using computers to calculate wind speed and direction. **10** **B** *Bees, on the other hand, do the same thing by checking the position of the sun and watching how the ground appears to be moving below them.* If the wind is affecting the way they are going, they change direction.

During this experiment, the researchers also discovered that the wind speed affects the height at which bees fly. On windy days, it appears, bees flying against the wind tend to fly lower than usual. **11** **H** *This, they found, is because it normally blows more strongly higher up.* Bees flying in the same direction as the wind, however, can use this to save energy by flying at greater heights.

Advice

9 Look for words like *one*, *do* and *so* used to link ideas, e.g. *There were six cakes. I ate one*; *They love surfing. I do, too*; *He says it's a good idea. I don't think so.*

10 Underline vocabulary links, e.g. use of the same word in both main text and sentence, or words with similar or opposite meanings.

11 When you see a word like *that* or *it*, decide what it refers to. Remember that it may refer backwards or forwards in the text.

3 Gaps 10 and 11 have also been completed with the correct sentence. Underline the expressions that link text and sentence.

Test 1 Exam practice — Reading Part 2

Action plan

1. Read the instructions, the title and any background information. What kind of text is it? What's the topic?
2. Quickly read through the main text. What is each paragraph about?
3. Look quickly at sentences A–H. Do any of them obviously fit particular gaps?
4. For each gap 9–15, study the ideas and words that come before and after it.
5. Look for similar or contrasting ideas in the list of sentences.
6. In both the main text and sentences A–H, underline vocabulary links, reference words such as *this* or *her*, and linking expressions like *also*, *even though*, *one*, *do* and *so*.

Tip! Before you choose a sentence, check that the verb forms, singular/plural, etc. in the main text all agree.

7. When you have chosen your answers, read the complete text. Does it make sense?

Tip! Each time you choose one of A–H, cross it out so that you don't have to keep reading through the whole list. This will save you time.

---

1 Look quickly at the exam task on page 16.
  1. What kind of text is it and what is it about?
  2. What is each of the main paragraphs about?

2 Follow the exam instructions, using the advice to help you.

A	Once you manage to find a more worthwhile website, however, there are real advantages.	**E**	Others require a large joining fee in order to progress to more advanced activities.
B	Of course, it's not easy to include exercise in your daily routine if you are lazy and spend all day sitting around at home.	**F**	Because of the amount of time they spend on the Internet, many of these people are actually doing less exercise than before.
C	Best of all, you can do so with the support of an online community who have the same aims as you.	**G**	Good eating habits are essential for achieving this, particularly if you want your weight to decrease, or increase.
D	Otherwise it's just too easy to give up, because you've paid nothing and nobody cares if you log onto (or off) the website, or whether you actually do any exercise at all.	**H**	True, but it can be hard to know exactly what that is when there is such an enormous range of online choice.

You are going to read an article about fitness websites on the Internet. Seven sentences have been removed from the article. Choose from the sentences **A–H** on page 15 the one which fits each gap (**9–15**). There is one extra sentence which you do not need to use.

The benefits of online fitness training

Thanks to the Internet you can now get into shape dressed in your pyjamas. By Lucy Atkins

Fitness experts these days generally agree that 'natural exercise' is the answer to our unhealthy lifestyles. An activity such as stair-climbing or running for the bus, they say, gets the heart rate going for five or ten minutes, several times a day, without the boredom of going to a gym or jogging round the park.

9 But thanks to the Internet it is now at least theoretically possible to get into great shape without even changing out of your pyjamas. The web is packed with creative, instant and varied exercises that are often available free. Just start typing and watch the kilos disappear.

Joanna Hall is a fitness expert who has set up a walking club on the Internet. At her *Walkactive* website, she promises that in six weeks you can achieve a 25% increase in fitness levels by following her activity programme based entirely on walking. 'These days people are used to finding what they need online,' she says. **10** Perhaps the best way to deal with this problem is just to have a look around and see what's out there.

One click of your mouse can take you, for instance, straight into an aerobics, dance or yoga class, or introduce you to a variety of other lively activities. You can put together your own strength training programmes, concentrate on particularly weak body parts or learn fun new ways of getting fit. **11** There are so many possibilities that you could spend the entire day sitting on your chair just surfing the websites and chatting with all these new friends you have made.

Quality, however, can be harder to find. Some sites try to tempt you into buying DVDs after they've started you off with free beginners' programmes. **12** Sometimes the quality of the picture or the sound can be extremely poor. You may have to put up with advertisements that suddenly appear on the screen, and there is the annoying tendency of some computers suddenly to pause in the middle of an activity, then return to the beginning of the video when you start clicking the mouse.

13 'Online programmes allow you to fit your training times around other things you have to do, such as going to college or work,' says Hall. 'They can be a very effective and achievable way to exercise, something you can do all year round.' You can use them any time of the day or night, in an office, hotel room or at home. In addition, you do not have to turn up at a gym or studio on time, wear embarrassing clothing, or deal with annoyingly fit people.

If a particular fitness programme doesn't completely suit you, the website may suggest ways of adjusting it to your own needs. It should also, most importantly, offer advice on healthier living in general. **14** Some sites will help you bring this about by providing charts showing how much change you can expect for a given amount of exercise. They may even encourage you to keep to your training programme by sending you regular emails, perhaps including a daily 'fit tip'.

All that is fine, but the trouble is that you do also need to have a certain amount of self-discipline to ensure that you keep going once you have started. **15** There's also the danger that family, friends or colleagues could come in and start laughing at you at any time. And there is a risk of injury if you don't follow the more complex instructions (though this issue arises with exercise DVDs and poorly taught classes too). Still, if you want a cheap, possibly funny and definitely varied way to get fit, then sit back and surf.

Advice

9 Look at the paragraphs before and after. Which sentence could refer back to 'stair-climbing' and 'running for the bus'? Where do people wear 'pyjamas'?

10 The sentence before mentions 'what they need'. Which sentence has a reference word linking back to this? Which describes a 'problem' with internet research?

11 This paragraph mentions lots of good things. Look for an expression that introduces something even better.

12 The sentence before the gap begins 'Some'. Which of A–H begins with a word that contrasts with this? The sentence needs to be another negative point about websites.

13 The previous paragraph describes bad websites. Which sentence mentions good ones, with a linking word showing contrast?

14 Look for a sentence with a reference word linking back to 'healthier living'. Does it also describe 'change'?

15 Which sentence gives reasons why you may not 'keep going'?

Test 1 Training — Reading Part 3

Task information

- In Part 3, there may be one long text divided into sections or a number of shorter texts.
- There are 15 questions which you match with the sections or short texts (**A**, **B**, **C**, etc.), according to the question at the top, e.g. *Which person or people ....*
- Part 3 tests your ability to find particular information in a text. You need to understand detail, attitudes and opinions in the questions, and find the part(s) of the text which express the same idea.
- The instructions tell you what kind of text it is and what it's about. It always has a title.
- You may be able to choose more than one option for some questions. If so, there will be extra spaces, e.g. 18 and 19, next to the question.
- The information you need may not be in the same order as the questions.

Finding evidence; avoiding incorrect answers

1 Study questions 16–21 on page 18 and extract C from a Part 3 text below. Match the underlined text with the correct question (17, 18 and 20) by drawing a line.

> **Tip!** There may be evidence for a particular answer in more than one sentence, or part of a sentence.

Which person

took up this means of transport for environmental reasons?	16 ....
feels that travelling this way is more comfortable than it was?	17 ....C.....
once arrived late at work because of transport delays?	18 ....C.....
dislikes having to travel surrounded by a lot of people?	19 ....
has to walk a considerable distance every day?	20 ....C.....
thinks they pay too much to travel to and from work?	21 ....

2 Look at questions 16, 19 and 21. Which two are answered correctly by extract E below? Underline the parts of the text that tell you, and write the question numbers on the right. Which is not answered correctly by E? How do you know?

> **C** Shop assistant Laura Sánchez recently switched from the bus to the tram to get to work. 'I wasn't keen at first,' she says, 'because <u>the nearest stop is more than a mile from my house, and that's quite a long way on foot</u> twice a day. I also used to think that <u>trams were cold, noisy things with hard wooden seats, but when I saw how much nicer they are these days,</u> I decided to make the change. The only problem,' she adds, 'is that if one breaks down there's a complete tram jam. <u>One Monday morning I was stuck like that for over an hour, and my boss wasn't pleased.</u>'
>
> 17
> 18
> 20

> **E** Justin Mackenzie works in the city centre and takes the train every day. 'It's handy for the office,' he says, 'but the fares keep going up and up and at this rate I'll have to think about using my car to come into town.' He thinks that would be 'crazy', pointing out that 'it was because of all the pollution it caused' that he gave up driving to work and started going by rail instead. 'I really wouldn't want to have to do that,' he says, adding: 'I don't even mind the fact that the rush-hour trains are so crowded, because at least it means there are fewer people using their cars.'

Test 1 Exam practice — Reading Part 3

Action plan

1 Read the instructions and the title to find out what kind of text it is and the topic.
2 Quickly read the questions underlining the key words.
3 Go quickly through the first section to see which questions it answers.
4 When you find information that seems to answer a question, read the question again and study the evidence in the text carefully.

Tip! Different texts or parts of the text may contain similar ideas, but you have to read carefully to decide which say **exactly the same thing** as the questions.

Follow the exam instructions, using the advice to help you.

You are going to read a magazine article about people who stayed in tree houses. For questions **16–30**, choose from the people (**A–D**). The people may be chosen more than once.

Which person

says they probably would not stay in a tree house again?	16
was sometimes keen to get back to the tree house?	17
was glad there was protection from insects?	18
enjoyed the view from the tree house?	19
did not have to walk up to the house?	20
took part in water sports?	21
liked the fact that local people benefit from the tree houses?	22
immediately accepted an unexpected offer?	23
spent a lot of time walking?	24
had stayed in a tree house before?	25
was pleasantly surprised by the local food?	26
wishes they had gone there as a child?	27
felt hot despite the cooling system?	28
was in a house with clean water from the ground?	29
regretted not taking something with them?	30

Advice

16 There's no need to read the whole text first. It's quicker to read the questions, then go through each section in turn. Look for another way of saying 'probably would not ... again'.

17 Think of a phrasal verb that means 'feel happy thinking about'.

18 Look for a type of insect, but be careful: one person had no 'protection' from them.

19 Make sure you choose the person who liked the view 'from' the house, not 'of' it.

20 What can you take to go up to an apartment? Look for this word, then read the next sentence.

21 All four people talk about water, but only one mentions actual 'water sports'.

22 Look for ways in which 'local people' are employed.

Tip! Don't expect to find answers in the text that use the same words as the questions. Look for words, phrases and sentences that express the same ideas.

Tip! You will need to use the same option for more than one question, e.g. four answers might all be A.

Holidays in a tree house

A

Primary-school teacher **Anisha Kapoor** went to the Green Magic Nature Resort in Kerala, south-west India. 'It wasn't my first experience of tree house living,' she says, 'but it was certainly the best. I was pleased to see that in a region where there aren't many jobs, the houses are entirely built and maintained by workers from the area, using traditional techniques and local materials. For instance, the lifts up to the front doors are made of cane grown in nearby fields. They work fine, by the way, and I was glad there were no stairs to climb – the houses are 25 metres up! That's good, though, because at that height there's often a cool breeze blowing through the branches. For power there's solar energy, and the taps in the kitchen and bathroom are supplied by pollution-free natural springs in the nearby hills. There's even a pretty good shower.'

B

Ever since TV researcher **Whitney Martin** worked on a programme about tree houses, she'd dreamt about staying in one. So when her neighbours happened to mention they had just such a place in Alaska, and asked whether she'd like to spend a fortnight there in July, she said 'yes' without a moment's hesitation. 'I couldn't believe it when I saw it,' she says, 'it had everything: even hot running water and cable TV. Though I rarely watched that because I was out most of the time. Just a few steps from the house there were trails that seemed to go on forever through the forest to some really fantastic rivers and lakes. And of course that far north the days are really long in summer, so I could keep going until very late. I hardly ever felt cold, though, and on those occasions when I did, I had a nice warm place of my own to look forward to. The only disadvantage of being there at that time of the year was the huge number of mosquitoes. I must have been bitten a hundred times.'

C

Australian technician **Richie O'Hara** was a guest at the Hinchinbrook Island Wilderness Lodge, on an island off the north coast of tropical Queensland. 'The wooden tree house was quite comfortable,' he says, 'and they had all the advertised facilities such as running water and a fridge. Actually, I hadn't fully read the brochure, so when I arrived, I was surprised to find an internet connection in the house and I wished I'd brought my computer with me. Still, I found plenty of healthy things to do, like canoeing and diving, and in the evening I could sit in the living room looking out above the rainforest to the Pacific beyond. That was great. After a week or so, though, I was a little tired of the climb to and from the house, so I doubt whether I'd repeat the tree-top experience. But I'm sure kids would love it – it's just a pity I didn't go there when I was about ten!'

D

Medical student **Kirsty Hammond** spent a week in Tanzania's Lake Manyara National Park, at the Lake Manyara Tree Lodge. 'As we approached it,' she says, 'we glimpsed the buildings up among the branches, with the Great Rift Valley in the background. It was a wonderful sight. The houses were comfortable, too, with running water, a well-equipped bathroom and, fortunately, large mosquito nets above the beds – I'm very aware of the dangers if they bite you. I also liked the fact that almost everything was above ground, even the restaurant. To be honest, I'd had my doubts about some of the traditional meals I'd seen people eating, but once I tasted them I realised how good they were. The only problem there was the high night-time temperature: although my bedroom had an overhead fan, I didn't sleep very well. But generally I had a great time. There's some fantastic wildlife around, including tree-climbing lions – though perhaps luckily I didn't actually see any of those.'

Test 1 Training — PAPER 2 Writing Part 1

Task information

- Part 1 tests your ability to write a letter or email.
- You are given a letter or email with notes on it. In your reply of 120–150 words you must include all the information it asks for.
- You have about 40 minutes for this task, including time at the end to check your work.
- You have to organise your text into paragraphs, with a suitable beginning and ending.
- You must write in an appropriate style, formal or informal, depending on who your text is for.
- You need to write full, grammatically correct sentences with correct punctuation and spelling, and use a good range of language.
- To find out how your writing will be assessed, go to the Cambridge ESOL website: http://www.cambridgeesol.org/assets/pdf/resources/teacher/fce_hb_dec08.pdf, page 28.

Useful language: formal and informal expressions

1 Decide whether A or B is more common in formal or informal writing.

1 A a friendly, personal tone ....informal....
   B a distant, impersonal tone ....formal....
2 A long words: *communicate* ....
   B short words: *chat* ....
3 A common words: *secret* ....
   B less common words: *confidential* ....
4 A active verb forms: *we gave* ....
   B passive verb forms: *we were given* ....
5 A phrasal verbs: *go on* ....
   B single-word verbs: *continue* ....
6 A full forms: *does not* ....
   B contracted forms: *doesn't* ....
7 A textbook expressions: *a limited quantity* ....
   B conversational expressions: *a bit* ....
8 A full forms of words: *especially* ....
   B abbreviations: *esp.* ....
9 A complete sentences: *I was extremely surprised.* ....
   B incomplete sentences: *Quite a shock.* ....
10 A use of exclamation marks: *I'm really happy!* ....
   B no exclamation marks: *I am extremely pleased.* ....

2 Decide whether each of these expressions is formal or informal and whether it usually goes at the beginning or the end of a letter.

Example: **Give my love to everyone.** *informal/end*

~~Give my love to everyone.~~	Yours sincerely,	Thanks (very much) for your letter.
This is just a quick note to say …	Dear Sir/Madam,	I apologise for the delay in replying.
It was great to get your email.	Best wishes,	Don't forget to write soon.
I have received your letter dated May 23.	Lots of love,	I look forward to hearing from you.
Well, that's all for now.	Dear Ben,	Hi Abbie
Sorry to be so slow getting back to you.		

3 Match the headings with groups of expressions 1–6. In each group there is one expression that is too formal for writing to a friend. Which is it?

Advising	~~Apologising~~
Changing the subject	Expressing enthusiasm
Expressing surprise	Requesting information

1 ......Apologising......
   I would like to apologise for arriving so late.
   Sorry about forgetting to tell you.
   Please forgive me for making that mistake.
   It was silly of me to suggest that.

2 ....
   Could you let me know what time you'll be here?
   I would be grateful if you could tell me the cost.
   I'd like to know if you've got a spare ticket.
   Can you give me an idea when it'll finish?

3 ....
   It'd be a good idea to try again.
   If I were you, I'd tell her now.
   My advice to you is to consider it most carefully.
   I really think you should go somewhere else.

4 ....
   By the way, what's his name?
   That reminds me, it's her birthday next week.
   With reference to the accommodation, there are certain changes …
   Anyway, how's life in general?

5 ....
   You'll never believe this, but she's his cousin!
   I was most surprised to discover that the price has risen.
   Funnily enough, we were both at the same primary school.
   Believe it or not, I've just won the lottery!

6 ....
   I'm delighted to hear you won a prize!
   It's a really exciting place to go with friends!
   I am extremely enthusiastic about learning Chinese.
   I think it's great that everyone will be there!

4 🔊 Read this letter written by a First Certificate candidate to a penfriend. It is well organised and there are no serious mistakes, but some of the expressions are too formal. Replace 1–8 with expressions from Exercise 2 on page 20 and Exercise 3 on this page.

Dear Emma,

(1) I am writing to you in reply to your letter. I'm very happy that you and your parents will stay in my country for a month.

(2) I believe it is a good idea that you will come to visit my city. I'm sure you will enjoy the holiday because

(3) it is an extremely interesting place to visit.

(4) In my opinion, I suggest that you go and hear music in one of the main squares in the city centre. I'm sure you will enjoy it. Moreover, there are a lot of cultural places to visit and history museums too.

(5) Next, I believe it would be better to come in the first part of the month, because that is when there are fewer tourists and fewer people visiting the monuments and the museums.

(6) To sum up, (7) I will be pleased to receive another letter from you soon, Emma.

(8) Yours sincerely,

Carlos

Writing Part 1

Understanding instructions; reading the text and notes

1 Look at these exam instructions.
   1 What kind of text has the candidate received?
   2 Who wrote it? What was her original plan?
   3 What does the candidate have to do?

> You have just received an email from your English-speaking friend, Lauren, who was going to meet you at the airport when you arrive in her country. Read Lauren's email and the notes you have made. Then write an email to Lauren, using **all** your notes.

2 Read Lauren's email and the notes next to it.
   1 What does she apologise for? What reason does she give?
   2 What two suggestions does she make in the second paragraph?
   3 What two suggestions does she make in the third paragraph?
   4 What does she suggest in the fourth paragraph? What does she ask?
   5 Has she written her email in a formal or an informal style? What examples can you find?

---

email

From:	Lauren Andrews
Sent:	12th April
Subject:	Airport arrival

I'm really sorry but I'm afraid it's impossible for me to meet you at the airport on Monday morning. They've just changed the date of my exam and I really have to be there till lunchtime. — *Doesn't matter, because …*

I think the best thing for you to do would be to take the train from the airport, and then we can meet in the city centre. — *Where and when?*

Then, if you like, we can find a nice little café in one of the quieter streets and have something to eat. Afterwards we can get the bus to my house.

No, because …

Yes, perhaps we could …

In the evening we can go out somewhere together. Is there anywhere you'd especially like to go?

I'm looking forward to seeing you!

Best wishes,
Lauren

---

22 | Test 1 Training　　　　　　　　　　　　　　　　　　　　　　　　　Writing Part 1

Test 1 Exam practice — Writing Part 1

Action plan

1 Read the instructions, the text and the notes beside it. Is the task a letter or an email?

Tip! Remember that we often use more formal language in letters than in emails.

2 Who do you have to write to? Why? Which points must you include? Decide whether to use formal or informal expressions.

3 Think about the topic and your reader, and note down ideas. How many paragraphs will you need?

4 Make a plan, put your best ideas under short paragraph headings. Do they cover all the points in the notes?

5 Note down some words or phrases for each paragraph, including expressions from the *Useful language* on pages 20–21, but don't try to write a complete draft.

6 Write your text, keeping to the topic and to your plan. Include one or two sentences about each of the notes.

7 Use a wide range of vocabulary and grammar, and make sure your handwriting is easy to read.

8 Check your completed text. Have you made any careless mistakes? Is it at least 120 words? If not, you will lose marks.

---

1 Look at the exam task below.

1 Is Adam's letter written in a formal or an informal style?
2 What does Adam tell you about the bike?
3 What five things does Adam ask you?
4 What two things do you need to ask Adam?
5 How many words must you write?

You **must** answer this question. Write your answer in **120–150** words in an appropriate style.

Your English-speaking friend, Adam, has just bought a mountain bike like yours. Read Adam's letter and the notes you have made. Then write a letter to Adam using **all** your notes.

> *Believe it or not, I won a mountain bike on an internet auction site for almost nothing! I've now picked it up from the seller, so shall we go out for a ride together this weekend?* — Yes, great idea!
>
> *I could go either on Saturday or Sunday. Which would suit you better?* — Say which, and why
>
> *I think it must be much more fun to ride off-road, so how about going into the countryside?* — Ask where, and how far
>
> *I really hope we can spend all day out riding. If so, do you think we should take some food with us? What kind would be best?* — Yes, suggest …
>
> *Please write back soon!*
>
> *All the best,*
>
> *Adam*

Tip! Use your own words instead of expressions taken from the text or the hand-written notes, e.g. if it says *What's your opinion?*, write *my own feeling is …* or *I'd say …* .

Tip! If you make any mistakes, cross them out and write the corrections. It doesn't matter if you make a lot of corrections, as long as they are easy to read.

Tip! You may lose marks if you use the same expression all the time. For instance instead of repeating *I want to*, say *I'd like to, what I'd enjoy is* or *it'd be good to …* .

Write your **letter**. You must use grammatically correct sentences with accurate spelling and punctuation in a style appropriate for the situation.

2 Follow the exam instructions and write your letter. Remember to check your work for mistakes when you finish.

Test 1 Training — Writing Part 2 (letter)

Writing Part 2 information

In Part 2 (questions 2–4) you choose one writing task. The possible tasks are: letter, essay, article (these three are practised on pages 27, 31 and 34), report, review, short story or task about set texts (these are practised on pages 78, 81, 84 and 85).

Task information (letter)

- The letter task in Part 2 tests your ability to write, for example, a formal job application or an informal letter giving information to a friend. You must write in an appropriate style.

- The instructions include a description of a situation. In response to this situation, you have to write a letter of between 120 and 180 words.
- You should allow about 40 minutes for this task, including time at the end to check your work.
- You have to organise your text into paragraphs, with a suitable beginning and ending.
- You should write full sentences with correct grammar and punctuation, using a good range of language with accurate spelling.

Useful language: formal expressions

Complete the formal expressions with the words given.

1 Giving a reason for writing

| apply   saw   reply   writing |

- a I am .... to inform you of a serious incident.
- b I would like to .... for the position of trainee chef.
- c I recently .... your advertisement in the newspaper.
- d In .... to your recent letter, I would like to make two points.

2 Describing yourself

| good   experience   knowledge   suitable |

- a I feel I would be .... for the job as I have the right skills.
- b I have a good .... of information technology.
- c I have had some .... of this kind of work.
- d I am particularly .... at solving problems.

3 Complaining

| disappointed   complain   pleased   complaint |

- a I wish to make a .... about the delay in delivery.
- b I am writing to .... about the service in your shop.
- c I was extremely .... with the item I bought.
- d I am not at all .... about the reply I received.

4 Requesting action

| like   please   grateful   must |

- a I would therefore .... you to investigate this matter.
- b I would be most .... if you could cancel my payment.
- c Would you .... ensure that this does not happen again.
- d I feel I .... ask you to make a formal written apology.

Text layout; formal & informal language; error correction

1 Look at the exam instructions below. Should you write in a formal or informal style?

You recently attended this event, but you did not enjoy it.

> **The perfect evening out!**
> - Top-class musical entertainment, with famous artists
> - Excellent restaurant
> - Discounts available for young people

Write your **letter of complaint** to the manager, saying what went wrong.

2 Look at this letter written by a First Certificate candidate. Find and correct the following (1–3):
1. poor layout. Where should it be divided into paragraphs?
2. two informal expressions, four contracted forms and four uses of informal punctuation.
   Change these to more formal language.
3. two mistakes each in verb forms, spelling and capital letters.
   Correct these.

Dear sir,

I'm writing to you to complain about the musical last night. I was looking forward to seeing your show but I have to say that it was a very disapointing evening. Firstly, my favourite singer Carmen Sánchez didn't perform, without any explanation being given. In addition, the show should started at 19.30, not 20.15! I was sure that discounts were available because I have read that they were, but the tickets office didn't offer them. So I had to pay full price for the ticket. What a terrible shock! After the show I was hungry so I went upstairs to the restaurant, but it was closed!

It certainly wasn't a perfect evening out so I want to have my money back!

Yours Faithfully,

Emilio Ricci

Writing Part 2 (letter)

3 Study the exam instructions below and the model letter written by Felipe, a very strong First Certificate candidate.
1 Is Felipe's letter the right length, and written in a suitable style?
2 Where does he deal with the three points in the advertisement?
3 What else does he say about himself?
4 What has he sent with his letter? Why?
5 What does he suggest to the employer?

You have seen this advertisement in an English-language newspaper.

> **CHILLI PEPPER CAFÉ**
> **Waiter/Waitress required**
>
> The person we are looking for will be:
> - good with people
> - prepared to work long hours
> - experienced in this kind of work
>
> Apply to the manager, Ms Harrison, saying why you are suitable for a job at our café.

Write your **letter of application**.

Dear Ms Harrison,

I wish to apply for the post of waiter at the Chilli Pepper Café, as advertised in the newspaper on October 22.

For the past two years I have been working at McDonald's and there I have gained wide experience in dealing with people. Cooking is the only hobby I have, and so I am very interested in different kinds of food. In view of the fact that I am used to working long hours, I believe I am ideally suited for this job.

Another reason for applying is that your café is only five minutes away from my home. Consequently, I would have only a short distance to travel every day.

I enclose a copy of my curriculum vitae, which will give you further details of my career to date.

I hope this information will be sufficient for you to consider my application. If you need further details, please do not hesitate to contact me. For an interview I could make myself available at any time.

I look forward to hearing from you.

Yours sincerely,

Felipe Martin

Annotations:
- Correct structure for current job
- Be polite to the employer
- Letter begins Dear Ms ...
- Say where you saw the ad
- Formal linking expressions
- Don't use 'will' until you get the job!
- Be helpful

26 | Test 1 Training

Writing Part 2 (letter)

Test 1 Exam practice — Writing Part 2 (letter)

Action plan

1 Study the instructions and the situation. Think about who you have to write to, why, and which points to include. Should you use formal or informal language?

2 Spend a few minutes making a plan, noting down all your ideas. How many paragraphs will you need?

3 Put your best ideas under paragraph headings. Also note down some words and phrases for each paragraph, including expressions from *Useful language* on page 24.

4 Write your text, keeping to the topic and to your plan. Use a wide range of vocabulary and grammar, and make sure your handwriting is easy to read.

Tip! You don't have to write any postal or email addresses in either Part 1 or Part 2.

5 Leave enough time at the end to check for mistakes – and that you have written at least 120 words.

Study the exam question and write your answer in 120–180 words in an appropriate style.

Tip! If you begin your letter *Dear Sir* or *Dear Madam*, end it *Yours faithfully*; if you use the person's surname, e.g. *Dear Ms Kay*, end with *Yours sincerely*.

You have seen this advertisement placed by the Tourist Information Office.

Summer tourist guides required

- Do you speak English?
- Do you like meeting people?
- Do you know your own town or city well?

If you can answer 'yes' to all these questions, apply to the manager, Ms Evans, explaining why you think you would be a good tourist guide.

Write your **letter of application**.

Test 1 Training — Writing Part 2 (essay)

Task information (essay)

- The essay task in Part 2 tests your ability to write an 'opinion' essay for the teacher of an English class.
- You are given a statement and you can choose to agree or disagree with it, or discuss the arguments both for and against it. You should write between 120 and 180 words.
- You should allow about 40 minutes for this task, including time at the end to check your work.
- Your essay must be well organised into paragraphs, with good linking expressions.
- As your reader will be the teacher, you should use fairly formal language.
- You should write full sentences with correct grammar and punctuation, using a good range of language with accurate spelling.

Useful language: ordering points or reasons; adding information

1 Where would you use these linking expressions? Put them under the correct headings.

In conclusion,	Next,	~~Firstly,~~
Last but not least,	Then	To begin with,
To sum up,	Secondly,	Lastly,
On balance,	Finally,	First of all,
To conclude,		

for the first point	for further points	for the last point	in the conclusion
Firstly			

2 Some linking expressions are used at the beginning of a sentence, some are not. Circle the correct words in *italics*.

1 In the city there are more places to go. *Also/Too*, they stay open later.
2 Working in a coal mine is a hard job. *Furthermore/As well*, it can be dangerous.
3 Travelling by train is more relaxing than driving. It is better for the environment, *besides/too*.
4 You have to find somewhere to play. *As well/As well as that*, you need to buy all the sports equipment.
5 In winter, the nights are much longer. *Too/In addition*, it is a lot colder then.
6 Making your own furniture is an enjoyable hobby. It saves money, *as well/in addition*.

Focusing on a statement; text organisation

1   Look at this exam task. Do you agree or disagree with the statement?

> You have had a class discussion on the subject of animals. Your teacher has now asked you to write an essay giving your opinion on the following statement.
>
> *It is cruel to keep animals in zoos.*
>
> Write your **essay**.

2   👁 Quickly read the essays on page 30 written by strong First Certificate candidates, A and B (language errors have been corrected). Ignore the gaps for the moment. Decide whether each essay includes:

- only arguments in favour of the statement
- only arguments against the statement
- arguments both for and against the statement

3   Now read the essays again and complete questions 1–10 with the following notes. You can use the same note more than once.

- Writer's own opinion
- Gives an example
- Sums up points already made
- Expression that links points
- Gives a reason
- Tells the reader what to expect
- Contrast link

Writing Part 2 (essay)   Test 1 Training | 29

Essay A

Writer's own opinion — In my opinion, keeping animals in zoos is not as cruel as people say – sometimes it is even useful – for three main reasons. — **(1)** Tells the reader what to expect

First of all, they take care of the animals, giving them the best food. The animals are cleaned every day and they live in good conditions. There is a large number of scientists that care for the animals, for instance if they catch a disease. — **(2)** ....

Gives a reason — Secondly there are some animals that are disappearing because they have been hunted without any control. At the zoo they are away from these hunters, so they are safe and it is possible to prevent them disappearing.

(3) .... — Finally there is also an educational reason. Children can see different animals from all over the world alive and from my point of view this is the best way of learning. They also learn to take care of them and the most important thing, to love them.

(4) .... — In conclusion, I believe keeping animals in a zoo is no more cruel than keeping them at home. The only important thing is to care for them. — Sums up points already made

Essay B

Outlines the background — Keeping animals in zoos is an important issue today because there are many people in favour of animal rights. In this essay I intend to examine the arguments for and against keeping animals in zoos. — **(5)** ....

Gives a reason — One of the strongest arguments in favour is the fact that children can see animals from other countries. Consequently, visiting zoos can help them learn about nature. Another advantage is that it can help protect some kinds of animals, which might be in danger of extinction. Furthermore, it is good entertainment for people. — Says which side comes first / **(6)** ....

(7) .... — On the other hand, there are several arguments against it. To begin with, it is known that animals in zoos suffer from loneliness since they are not living in their natural environment. Secondly, they do not behave as they would do if they were free, because they have to get used to a new way of living, even if they have been born in the zoo. Lastly, people can use them to carry out experiments.

(8) ....

(9) .... — On balance, I am not in favour of keeping animals in captivity because, as I have shown, that is like prison, which is very sad. — **(10)** ....

30 | Test 1 Training Writing Part 2 (essay)

Test 1 Exam practice — Writing Part 2 (essay)

Action plan

1 Read the instructions and the statement. Do you agree with it?

2 Decide whether to write for or against the statement, or whether to give arguments both for *and* against.

Tip! Choose the essay option in Part 2 if you have strong feelings about the topic.

3 Spend a few minutes making a plan. If you are going to write for *and* against, list your points in two columns so you can balance the essay.

4 Write a short introductory paragraph, commenting generally on the topic, e.g. *The climate is changing, so many people are saying ...* . You can give your own opinion here and/or in your last paragraph.

5 Write in a fairly formal style, including linking expressions from *Useful language* on page 28.

6 Write a paragraph for each main point, giving reasons and possibly also examples.

7 Give your opinion by summarising your main points in a concluding paragraph.

8 Check your essay for mistakes – and that you have written at least 120 words.

Study the exam question and write your answer in 120–180 words in an appropriate style.

Tip! In a 'for and against' essay, it is usually clearer to write the 'for' paragraphs first and then the 'against' paragraphs, before concluding.

Tip! If you want to think of points you disagree with, imagine what someone who disagrees would say.

You have had a class discussion on TV programmes. Now your English teacher has asked you to write an essay, giving your opinion on the following statement:

There is far too much sport on television.

Write your **essay**.

Test 1 Training — Writing Part 2 (article)

Task information (article)

- The article task in Part 2 tests your ability to write an interesting text for a magazine or newsletter.
- You may need to write descriptions, give examples, make comments or give your opinions.
- You are writing for readers who are already interested in the topic.
- You should write **120–180** words.

Useful language: strong expressions

1 You can make your writing more interesting by using stronger expressions. Replace the words in *italics* with the adjectives in the box.

awful	enormous	essential	exhausted	fantastic
fascinated	filthy	freezing	furious	terrified

1 By midnight, we were completely *tired*.
2 When I found out about it, I was *angry* with her.
3 The water was *cold*, so Holly swam quickly.
4 We all had a really *good* day at the theme park.
5 Matt was *afraid*, but he tried not to show it.
6 There are two *big* mountains on the island.
7 After playing rugby, Joe's shirt was *dirty*.
8 That nightclub is *bad*, the worst in town.
9 When you go diving, it is *important* to stay safe.
10 Visitors are *interested* by the ancient drawings.

2 Write a sentence of your own, using each of the words in the box.

Focusing on instructions

1 Look at this exam task. What two things does the writer have to do?

You have seen this announcement on an English-language website.

> **My favourite sport**
>
> Tell us why you enjoy your favourite sport so much, and what people should do if they want to take it up.
>
> We will publish the most interesting articles in the next few days.

Write your **article**.

2 Study these two articles written by First Certificate candidates (language errors have been corrected). For each question 1–12, write *Yes* or *No* under A, B or both A and B. Where possible, give a reason or example.

Which article	A	B
1 has an interesting title and introduction?	No. Title too similar to task, dull introduction.	Yes. They catch readers' attention.
2 deals with both parts of the task?		
3 is well organised into paragraphs?		
4 is written in an informal style?		
5 makes good use of linking words?		
6 uses a good range of vocabulary?		
7 uses a good range of structures?		
8 gives relevant examples?		
9 includes the writer's opinions?		
10 describes personal experiences?		
11 asks the reader a question?		
12 has an interesting ending?		

3 Which article, A or B, got a better mark, do you think?

Article A

MY CHOICE OF SPORT

In this article I would like to explain why I decided, one day, to take up a certain sport. First of all, doing some sport is good for your health. This is obvious, but which kind of sport suits you? If you want to combine exercise with enjoyment, I can recommend volleyball.

One advantage is that you can play in a team, which can be really fantastic!

Also, volleyball is never boring, compared to endless hours in the gym.

For me, this game is an art where you have to use your skill and brain as well!

The main advice to anyone who would like to try this sport is to protect your joints! You can get high-quality equipment for this sport everywhere.

Secondly, you have to be cooperative with your teammates.

Last but not least, enjoy yourself!

Article B

DIVING DEEP

Are you too scared to try something new, something unusual which involves more risk than everyday sports? If not, go diving – you'll love it.

I am a 21-year-old girl and I've been scuba-diving for three years. It's not just a hobby for me; it's much more than that.

At first everybody is terrified of sinking into a deep, dark sea, because anything can happen, at any time. But you can't keep thinking about this, otherwise you'll miss a different, magical world down there.

Everybody says you can see all that on TV, but it's not the same. You have to see everything with your own eyes. It's wonderful when you discover something you have never seen before, such as a shark swimming. It is unbelievable.

I suggest everyone try scuba-diving at least once. It needs practice, maybe for three weeks, to be good at it, but a good instructor can help. You also have to buy your equipment. Ask somebody to help you if you don't know exactly what you need.

It's well worth it. I just know that everyone who decides to go scuba-diving will have a fantastic time!

Test 1 Exam practice — Writing Part 2 (article)

Action plan

1. Read the instructions. Do you know enough about the topic to write an article?
2. Think about who your readers are and what they would like to read about.
3. Spend a few minutes making a plan based on all parts of the task, noting down points and language for each paragraph. Try to include some adjectives from *Useful language* on page 32.
4. Think of a good title to attract your readers' attention, and an interesting introduction to make them want to keep reading.
5. Write your text in a lively way that will hold their interest. You can describe your own experiences and give your own opinions.
6. Use language that is fairly informal. Try to include some interesting expressions, e.g. *it's well worth it*, and perhaps questions like *I wonder what would happen if ...*
7. Make the ending interesting by encouraging readers to think about what they have read.
8. Check your article for mistakes – and that you have written at least 120 words.

Study the exam question and write your answer in 120–180 words in an appropriate style.

You recently saw this announcement in *Transport 2020* magazine.

Readers are invited to write articles about the following:

Transport in the Future

How do you think people will travel in the future? What changes will there be and what differences will these make to the way we live?

The writer of the best article will receive a cash prize.

Write your **article**.

Tip! Prepare yourself for this task by reading articles in English in magazines or on the Internet.

Test 1 Training — PAPER 3 Use of English Part 1

Task information

- In Part 1 you choose from words **A**, **B**, **C** or **D** to fill in each gap in a text. Options A, B, C and D are always the same kind of word (e.g. *verbs*).
- Part 1 mainly tests vocabulary but you may also need to understand grammatical links between words, or the text as a whole.
- Words that often go together, called 'collocations', are often tested and so are words followed by a preposition (e.g. *aware of*).

Tip! Prepare for this task by noting phrases formed with words that often go together (e.g. *ride a bike, loud noise*) in your vocabulary notebook.

Useful language: collocations

1 Match each noun in the box with the verbs below. (Some nouns go with more than one verb.) Then think of more nouns to add to each column.

a mistake	shopping	a party	a shower	swimming	a photo	skiing
a noise	the bus	some homework	a job	a break	friends
fun	the dishes	~~sports~~	riding	time	notes	progress

do	make	take	have	go
sports				

2 Note down as many nouns as you can that often go with each of these verbs.

| beat   catch   earn   hold   keep   lose   miss   pass   play   save   spend   win |

3 👁 Correct one mistake in sentences 1–10 written by First Certificate candidates, using verbs from Exercises 1 and 2.

1 We can meet and we can pass some time together!
2 If you want to get fun, I think it's better for you to go downtown.
3 You can make a lot of sports and activities with other people.
4 We can meet new people and know a few friends.
5 I have to give an exam at the university.
6 My friends are arriving next week so I'd like to make a party.
7 People make shopping in the nearest town and they spend a lot of money there.
8 Well as you can see I have made some photos of my room.
9 Please sit down and make your homework.
10 We went to a nice little café, took a coffee and talked.

4 Write each of these adjectives and verbs on the correct line or lines. Then think of more words for each line.

afraid	agree	apply	aware	belong	bound
care	depend	familiar	famous	interested	involved
jealous	keen	object	pleased	rely	succeed

1 _agree, belong, bound, object_ .... to   4 .... in

2 .... of   5 .... for

3 .... on   6 .... with

5 For each of sentences 1–10, choose the correct word, A, B, C or D.

1 This film is ... almost entirely on events that really happened.
   A set   B based   C rested   D fixed

2 Eventually the rescue team ... in finding the missing walkers.
   A managed   B achieved   C fulfilled   D succeeded

3 You can always ... on Simon to help you. He's a good friend.
   A rely   B trust   C bargain   D believe

4 The police still do not know who was ... for the theft.
   A guilty   B probable   C likely   D responsible

5 It wasn't her turn, but Hannah ... on paying for the drinks.
   A demanded   B required   C requested   D insisted

6 Some people are ... of the success of others.
   A angry   B jealous   C greedy   D dissatisfied

7 My grandparents don't ... of people who have bad manners.
   A respect   B admire   C approve   D appreciate

8 Marta wanted the gold medal and was not ... with silver.
   A glad   B cheerful   C satisfied   D positive

9 When I study medicine at university I want to ... in surgery.
   A specialise   B concentrate   C dedicate   D focus

10 This part of the country is ... for its beautiful scenery.
    A impressive   B proud   C famous   D outstanding

Test 1 Exam practice — Use of English Part 1

Action plan

1 Look at the title and the example.
2 Without filling in any gaps, quickly read the text to get an idea of what it's about.
3 For each gap, decide what kind of word (e.g. *nouns*, *adverbs*) the four options are.
4 Study the words either side of the gap, underlining any possible collocations.
5 Try each word in the gap, checking whether it fits the grammar of the sentence.
6 Check that the word you choose fits the overall meaning of the text.
7 Read through the complete text, checking that everything makes sense.

Follow the exam instructions on page 38, using the advice to help you.

Tip! Write the example answer into gap (0). It will help you understand the beginning of the text.

#	A	B	C	D
1	leading	resulting	causing	creating
2	pass	employ	use	spend
3	aware	thoughtful	wise	familiar
4	save	secure	guard	defend
5	liked	popular	approved	accepted
6	used	experienced	preferred	prepared
7	do	live	cause	have
8	positive	inevitable	bound	definite
9	eager	keen	fond	enthusiastic
10	going	cycling	playing	riding
11	meet	know	join	make
12	demand	apply	claim	order

Tip! If you're not sure of an answer, cross out any you know are wrong and choose from those remaining.

For questions **1–12**, read the text below and decide which answer (**A, B, C** or **D**) on page 37 best fits each gap. There is an example at the beginning (**0**).

Example:

0 **A** making   **B** taking   **C** travelling   **D** flying

| 0 | A | **B** | C | D |

Holidays at home

Official figures show that the number of people **(0)** .... international flights is decreasing, and that this is **(1)** .... in significant changes to holidaying habits.

As the cost of air tickets increases, it appears that more and more families are choosing to **(2)** .... their summer holidays at home. People are also becoming more **(3)** .... of the harm that flying does to the environment, and see it as a way of helping to **(4)** .... the planet, too.

For many parents a summer with no airport queues or overcrowded resorts may seem attractive, but the idea might well be less **(5)** .... with their teenage children, who are probably **(6)** .... to flying off to the Mediterranean or Miami as soon as school breaks up. So, the question is, how can young people **(7)** .... lots of fun when so much will be closed for the holidays, and so many of their friends are **(8)** .... to be away?

The answer may lie at the local sports centre. Nowadays, many centres organise summer activities aimed at young people **(9)** .... either on indoor or outdoor sports. These might range, for instance, from playing table tennis to **(10)** .... mountain-biking. As well as being healthy and enjoyable, taking part in activities like these is also an excellent way to **(11)** .... new friends. For the most popular activities, though, it is advisable to **(12)** .... early for a place – perhaps two or three months in advance.

Advice

0 *The only word of the four that forms a collocation with 'flights' is 'taking'.*

2, 4, 7, 10, 11 *Which of A, B, C or D often goes with this noun? Notice that it isn't always next to the gap.*

1, 3, 5, 6, 9, 12 *Which of A, B, C or D goes with this preposition and fits the meaning of the text? Notice that it isn't always next to the gap.*

9, 12 *Which of A, B, C or D goes with this preposition and fits the meaning of the text? Notice that it isn't always next to the gap.*

10, 11 *Which of A, B, C or D often goes with this noun? Notice that it isn't always next to the gap.*

Tip! Fill in your answers on the question paper in pencil. This will help you check the completed text when you finish.

Test 1 Training — Use of English Part 2

Task information

- In Part 2 there is a text with 12 gaps. There are no sets of words from which to choose.
- Part 2 mainly tests 'grammar words' like articles (e.g. *the*, *an*), auxiliary verbs (e.g. *will*, *has*), pronouns (e.g. *they*, *who*), prepositions (e.g. *on*, *during*), linking expressions (e.g. *despite*) and verb forms (e.g. *would do*), as well as words in phrasal verbs (e.g. *set off*) and fixed phrases (e.g. *in favour of*).
- You must only use one word in each gap and your spelling must be correct.

Useful language: relative pronouns and linking expressions

1 Questions in Part 2 sometimes focus on relative pronouns like *which*. Complete these rules with the words in the box.

| that | when | where | which | who | whose |

Rules
In any kind of relative clause, we can use **(1)** .... for people, **(2)** .... for things, **(3)** .... for possession, **(4)** .... for time and **(5)** .... for places. In a defining relative clause we can also use **(6)** .... for people or things, e.g. *the girl* **(7)** .... *sang really well*; *the tree* **(8)** .... *grew so tall*.

2 Tick ✔ the sentences which are correct and replace the relative pronoun in those that are wrong. Sometimes more than one answer is possible.
1. It's a huge city, when one can find a lot of different kinds of people.
2. The weather was hot except on the first day, that it was windy.
3. John wasn't sure if the person which he saw was his brother Mike.
4. I prefer to stay in the countryside, what I think is better.
5. There are some people whose aim in life is to earn as much money as possible.
6. I met an interesting boy there, Carlos, that is a good singer and is also handsome!
7. I gave the money to an organisation who helps poor children.
8. They invited me to a pop concert which took place in Rio last month.
9. So we went to Tetuan, that is a little city in the north of Morocco.
10. He's a man who's life story is the greatest book that has been written in the last 50 years.

3 Complete the text using relative pronouns.

Melanie Johnson, **(1)** .... house is opposite mine, is my favourite neighbour. She's a warm and friendly person **(2)** .... always likes to help other people. In the afternoon, **(3)** .... I come home, she often waves and smiles to me from her front garden, **(4)** .... she spends a lot of time in spring and summer. It has some lovely flowers, **(5)** .... she planted herself, and last week she gave some to my mother, **(6)** .... birthday was on Friday. She's always been generous like that. I remember years ago, **(7)** .... I was about ten, she painted a picture for me **(8)** .... was so lovely that I put it on my bedroom wall. It's still there.

Tip! You always have to fill in the gap in Part 2. The missing word can never be left out of the sentence.

4 Some questions in Part 2 test linking expressions like *although* or *unless*. Put the words and expressions in the box under the correct heading below.

although	so	on account of	~~and~~
despite (the fact that)	due to (the fact that)	in order to	~~because~~
provided (that)	as well as	~~but~~	(and) yet
though	unless	in order that	whereas
~~if~~	as long as	even so	since
in case	besides	while	owing to
so as to	even though	~~to~~	in spite of
however	in addition to	because of	

reason	contrast	purpose	addition	conditional
because	but	to	and	if

5 In these sentences written by First Certificate candidates, circle the correct alternative in *italics*.

1. The city is unhealthy *because/because of* the pollution in the air.
2. *Although/In spite of* these problems, would you still like to invite me next month?
3. *Unless/Besides* you live in a big town, there are no traffic jams.
4. Please do not hesitate to contact me *if/in case* you need more detailed information.
5. I think that people should use their bicycles *so/so as to* reduce traffic.
6. I hope you will stay at our house *in order/in order that* you can visit our country.
7. The green hills and valleys need protecting *because/owing to* many people are building modern houses.
8. The other staff patiently explained the job to me *even though/even so* they were very busy themselves.
9. *Since/As long as* I love swimming and your club seems to be suitable, I would like to join it.
10. There are many ways of getting to school *in case/if* you study far away from your neighbourhood.

6 Complete the text with words from Exercise 4. Sometimes more than one answer is possible.

It was getting late by the time Sam and Marco approached the summit, on **(1)** .account. of the terrible weather on their way up. In **(2)** .... to high winds that nearly swept them right off the mountain, they faced freezing temperatures and heavy snowfalls. And **(3)** .... neither of them had any thoughts of giving up. In **(4)** .... of the awful conditions they were determined to keep climbing even **(5)** .... every step was now a huge effort, **(6)** .... to the fact they were so high up and the air was so thin. As **(7)** .... as that, Marco was feeling quite ill, probably **(8)** .... of the height and a lack of food. But they knew that **(9)** .... reach the top they couldn't stop for anything, even meals. They also knew that **(10)** .... they got there this time, they would probably never have another chance to try. And Sam was sure that as **(11)** .... as they could begin going down by three o'clock, they would make it safely back to base camp tonight – **(12)** .... they would both be very, very tired.

Tip! Answers are never hyphenated words such as *old-fashioned*.

Test 1 Exam practice — Use of English Part 2

Action plan

1. Look at the title and the example.
2. Without trying to fill in any answers, quickly read the text to see what it's about.
3. For each gap, look at the context and decide what kind of word (e.g. *relative pronoun*) is needed.
4. Study the words either side of the gap for more clues.
5. Think of words that might fit and try each one.
6. When you have filled in all the gaps, read your text to check it makes sense.

Follow the exam instructions, using the advice to help you.

Tip! Gaps may have more than one possible answer, but you must only put one.

Tip! If you can't answer a particular question, go on to the others and come back to it later when you have completed more of the text.

For questions **13–24**, read the text below and think of the word which best fits each gap. Use only **one** word in each gap. There is an example at the beginning (**0**).

Example: 0 | W | H | I | C | H |

A short history of tattooing

Tattoos, (0) *which* some people call 'body art', have become more and more popular in recent years. In (13) .... of the pain caused by having a needle make hundreds of holes in their skin, millions of people (14) .... vary widely in age and background are nowadays having their bodies decorated with ink in all kinds of ways.

Many of today's young people, (15) .... parents were the first generation to experiment with tattoos, see it as a way of expressing their individuality, and in (16) .... to do this, they are constantly looking for new styles and designs. (17) .... to this increasing demand, tattoo studios have appeared in many towns and villages.

(18) .... people tend to think of it as a modern practice, tattooing has in fact been around for a long time. There is evidence of tattoos being worn in Siberia over 4,000 years ago, as (19) .... as in Ancient Egypt at that time, and it is thought to have existed in Japan 10,000 years ago. Even (20) .... , it was not until the late 18th century, (21) .... Captain James Cook sailed to Polynesia, that Europeans took an interest.

It was on the island of Tahiti, (22) .... tattooing had an important role in society, that Cook and his crew first saw tattooed men and women, and (23) .... of that, the English word comes from the Tahitian word *tatau*. Ever since then, sailors have had tattoos done, often (24) .... show the distant places they have visited.

Tip! Never put contracted forms like *he's* or *won't* as they count as **two** words.

Advice

0 A relative pronoun is needed. Tattoos are things so it could be 'which' or 'that', but the commas show this is a non-defining relative clause so it must be 'which'.

13, 18, 20 Contrast link needed.

14, 15, 21, 22 Relative pronoun needed.

16, 24 Purpose link needed.

17, 23 Reason link needed.

19 Addition link needed.

Test 1 Training — Use of English Part 3

Task information

- In Part 3 you read a text containing 10 gaps. At the end of some lines there is a word in capital letters for you to form one appropriate word to fill each gap.
- Part 3 mainly tests your ability to form new words and different parts of speech.
- You may, for example, need to form adverbs by adding -ly to adjectives, make nouns plural by adding -s or -es, change verb/adjective forms by adding -ed or -ing, or form comparative/superlative forms by adding -er or -est.
- You may also have to make spelling changes (e.g. *long* to *length*). You must always get the spelling right to get a point!

Useful language: word formation

1 To do Part 3 successfully, you need to know which affixes are often used for different parts of speech. Match the prefixes and suffixes a–d with 1–4. Write an example for each.

a un- in- im- dis- ir-
b -er -ee -ist -ant -or
c -tion -ment -ness -ity
   -ance -ence -ship
d -ful -less -able -ous
   -ive -itive -y -ible

1 people who do jobs *b – bus driver, employee, artist, shop assistant, instructor*
2 negative prefixes (mainly used for adjectives but also some verbs and nouns)
3 adjective suffixes
4 noun suffixes

Tip! When you see words with affixes while you are reading in English, write them down in your vocabulary notebook.

2a Complete the table, using your dictionary if you need to. Use affixes from Exercise 1 and follow these spelling rules:

- For adjectives ending in -y, change the y to an i (e.g. *easy/easily*).
- With suffixes beginning with a vowel, drop the final e (e.g. *prepare/preparation*).
- For some words, you need to make other spelling changes (e.g. *high/height, freeze/frozen, little/least*).

b Where more than one word is possible, explain the difference, e.g. comfort – *pleasant*, discomfort – *unpleasant*.

verb	noun(s)	adjective(s)	adverb(s)
comfort	comfort(s), discomfort(s)	(un)comfortable	(un)comfortably
employ			
hope			
	noise(s), noisiness		
lose			
	science(s), scientist(s)		
relate			
succeed			

Tip! When you learn a word, use a good dictionary to find out which affixes you can add and how these change the meaning. Note these down, with example sentences.

3 Complete the sentences using the word in capitals. Use words from the table in Exercise 2.

1 Our neighbours are friendly so we have a good ......relationship...... with them. **RELATION**

2 Most .... agree that sea levels will continue to rise in the coming years. **SCIENCE**

3 The huge waterfall was so .... that I couldn't hear a word anyone said. **NOISE**

4 In an area of such high .... , we must provide new jobs for local people. **EMPLOY**

5 Our situation on the island seemed .... as we had no water or food left. **HOPE**

6 The 800-kilometre journey in an old bus with hard seats was very .... **COMFORT**

7 Our plan to save the trees was .... and sadly they have all now been cut down. **SUCCESS**

8 The .... of so much rainforest will have a terrible effect on the climate. **LOSE**

Advice

1 The article 'a' and the adjective 'good' mean we need a noun. If people are 'friendly' we probably get on well with them, so we have 'a good relation**ship**'.

2 The verb 'agree' needs a subject, probably a kind of people. It is plural so this noun must be plural, too.

3 The missing word describes 'waterfall' so it's an adjective. If the person 'couldn't hear' it means there was a lot of noise.

4 After the adjective 'high' we need a noun from 'employ'. If 'new jobs' are required, there can't be enough now, so the meaning will be negative.

5 The missing word describes 'situation' so it must be an adjective. That situation was clearly negative.

6 We need an adjective to describe the 'journey'. We must make comfort negative by adding both a suffix and a negative prefix.

7 The word 'sadly' shows it is a negative idea, so we need an adjective to describe 'plan' with a negative prefix.

8 After the article 'the' we need a noun meaning something lost, but we need to be careful with the spelling.

4 ⊙ These sentences written by First Certificate candidates each contain word formation errors. Correct the mistakes. Think about the spelling rules in Exercise 2 on page 42. Which of 1–10:
- use the wrong affix?
- have a spelling mistake?
- confuse singular and plural?

1 I think that going to school by bike is very healthful.
2 Your report about the music festival is absolutely inacceptable!
3 I am very worried about the increasing pollutions of the Earth.
4 Scientifics need to study animals so they study the ones at the zoo.
5 I think it was my first big disapointing, but it wasn't the last.
6 I visited many ancient Roman cities that are remarkable well preserved.
7 Most of the animals are loosing their natural instincts.
8 There was no central heatings and no bathroom.
9 In other countries there aren't so many accidents. We are very uncarefull here.
10 The bookshop needs employers for part-time or full-time jobs.

Use of English Part 3 | Test 1 Training | 43

Test 1 Exam practice — Use of English Part 3

Action plan

1 Quickly read the title and the text. What's it about?
2 Look at each word in CAPITALS and the words before and after the gap. Is the missing word likely to be a noun, a verb, or another part of speech?
3 If it's a noun, is it countable or uncountable?
4 If it's an adjective, is it positive or negative?
5 Does the word in CAPITALS need more than one change?
6 Check the word you have chosen fits the context and is spelt correctly.

1 Look at the example (0). What kind of word comes after 'the most' and before a noun? What suffix must you add to the verb *remark* to form this word?

2 Follow the exam instructions, using the advice to help you. Then follow the Action plan for questions 30–34.

For questions **25–34**, read the text below. Use the word given in capitals at the end of some of the lines to form a word that fits in the gap **in the same line**. There is an example at the beginning **(0)**.

Example: | 0 | R | E | M | A | R | K | A | B | L | E | | | |

India's rainforest by night

India has amazing countryside with some of the most **(0)** ..remarkable.. wildlife on Earth, and its 96 National Parks are becoming **(25)** .... popular. These parks contain a huge **(26)** .... of creatures, from multicoloured butterflies to magnificent tigers, but **(27)** .... for visitors, many of them are active mainly at night and then seem to **(28)** .... during the day. In southern India's Periyar National Park, however, they have found a solution to this problem: night tours.

Walking through the rainforest in the dark is a wonderful way to observe creatures in their natural **(29)** .... You quickly become more **(30)** .... to the sounds of birds and animals, and you soon begin to recognise some of their calls. You are accompanied by local guides to prevent you getting lost, and also for **(31)** .... reasons: there are big cats around, and **(32)** .... snakes, too.

Many visitors want to continue their **(33)** .... of the jungle all night, but if you want a break from the tropical **(34)** .... there are rivers where you can go for a cooling swim by moonlight.

REMARK
INCREASE
VARIOUS
FORTUNATE
APPEAR

SURROUND
SENSE

SAFE
POISON

EXPLORE
HOT

Advice

25 Adverbs often describe adjectives, so how can you make an adverb from the verb 'increase'?

26 Should the word after 'a' + adjective be countable or uncountable? Singular or plural? Be careful with the extra spelling change.

27 Is it good or bad for visitors that many animals are 'active mainly at night'? What prefix should you use?

28 What kind of word normally comes after 'to'? To contrast with 'active', is it likely to be positive or negative? What prefix do we need?

29 What kind of word is likely to follow the adjective 'natural'? Is it normally singular or plural?

Tip! When you have filled in all the gaps, read the complete text to make sure everything makes sense. Don't forget you need to make change(s) to ALL the words in capitals. Don't leave any unchanged!

3 For each of the words in capitals in the exam task, find other words that can be formed from it and add these to your vocabulary notebook, with example sentences.

Test 1 Training — Use of English Part 4

Task information

- In Part 4 there are eight questions each with a lead in sentence, a key word, and a second gapped sentence for you to complete.
- Part 4 tests grammar *and* vocabulary by asking you to use different structures and words to express the same idea.
- You have to write your answer in 2, 3, 4 or 5 words. This includes the word in capitals, which you have to use and mustn't change. You lose marks if you ignore any of these instructions.
- Each correct answer gets two marks, with one mark for each part of the answer, so Part 4 has more possible marks than other parts of Use of English.

Useful language: key word transformations

1 Part 4 sometimes focuses on expressions followed by the *-ing* form or *to* + infinitive. Study the rules and add the words in the box to the lists in 1–3. Then add three more examples to each.

likely	enjoy	carry on	without	it's no use	forget
help someone	easy	there's no point (in)	suggest	give up	after
want something	plan	stop	expect	avoid	it's not worth
despite	pleased	tell someone	decide	try	put off

Rules

1 We use the *-ing* form after
- some verbs (e.g. *it keeps raining*)
  Examples: ....
- prepositions (e.g. *I'm keen on riding*)
  Examples: ....
- two-part (and three-part) verbs (e.g. *I'm looking forward to meeting her*)
  Examples: ....
- some expressions (e.g. *I'm fed up with waiting*)
  Examples: ....

2 We use the *to* + infinitive form after
- some verbs (e.g. *I want to leave*)
  Examples: ....
- some verbs + object (e.g. *He asked me to go*)
  Examples: ....
- some adjectives (e.g. *I was glad to see* her)
  Examples: ....

3 We can use either *-ing* or *to* + infinitive after some verbs, but with different meanings, e.g. *I regret to tell* you (I'm sorry to tell you this), or *I regret telling* you (I'm sorry I told you).
  Examples: ....

2 Complete the second sentence so that it means the same as the first sentence, using the *-ing* or the *to* + infinitive form of the verb.

1 I'm going out this evening. — I've decided <u>to go out this evening.</u>
2 I like to listen to music in the evening. — I enjoy ....
3 The bus will probably be late again. — The bus is likely ....
4 We can't play tennis until Saturday. — We'll have to put off ....
5 It doesn't make sense to stay here. — There's no point in ....
6 Although I felt ill, I went to school. — Despite ....
7 I'll be glad if Mark comes to my party. — I want Mark ....
8 Kate didn't remember to call Emma. — Kate forgot ....

3 Correct these sentences written by First Certificate candidates.
1 I hope hearing from you soon.
2 We would suggest to replace the shopping trip on Tuesday with the castle visit.
3 And before to go to sleep, we had supper.
4 I rarely cook. It's much easier going to the supermarket for a ready-to-eat meal.
5 I am quite busy to prepare for my exam.
6 It's worth to go to the annual festival.
7 I am really interested in to work in your company.
8 The only doubt was if I could afford buying it this year.
9 I am looking forward to hear from you.
10 After I had driven about 50 km, the engine stopped to work.

4 Part 4 questions sometimes test past forms of modal verbs: modal + *have* + past participle (e.g. *There's no reply – she must have left already*). Make a list of other past modal forms and their negatives (e.g. *would have left / would not (wouldn't) have left*).

5 Use past modal forms to complete the second sentence so that it means the same as the first.

1 It's a pity you didn't arrive earlier.   You should ......*have arrived*...... earlier.
2 I'm sure Jack was happy when he saw his exam results.   Jack must .... happy when he saw his exam results.
3 It's possible that Zoe's friends didn't tell her.   Zoe's friends may .... her.
4 There's just a chance that Sean got you a ticket.   Sean might .... you a ticket.
5 I'm sure your parents weren't pleased when they saw the bill.   Your parents can't .... pleased when they saw the bill.
6 There was no need for you to get up early – go back to bed!   You needn't .... early – go back to bed!
7 Unfortunately, you sent in your application too late.   You should .... your application too late.
8 I'm sorry you didn't tell me about this before.   You ought .... me about this before.

6 In these sentences written by First Certificate candidates, circle the correct alternative in *italics*.
1 The programme *should have beginning/should have begun* at midday last Saturday.
2 I saw that somebody had opened the back door, but I didn't have any idea who it *might have been/might had been*.
3 The time that the show *should start/should have started* was 19.30 but it started 45 minutes later.
4 It was really wonderful and I *could have never/could never have* imagined it.
5 We *had not to/did not have to* pay for any accommodation there because a friend of Juan put us up.
6 Animals in zoos were not born where they *should have been/must have been* born: in their natural environment.
7 We *didn't need to/needn't to* go to the supermarket when we arrived at the apartment because there was already food there.
8 I *can't have/couldn't have* imagined until that day how difficult it is to live without electrical energy.

Test 1 Exam practice — Use of English Part 4

Action plan

1 Read the instructions and the example. This will remind you exactly what you have to do.

2 For each question, study both sentences and the key word in CAPITALS. What differences are there between the two sentences?

3 Decide what kind of word (e.g. *noun*) the key word is, and what often follows it (e.g. *preposition*).

4 Begin by thinking about what the question is testing (e.g. *conditionals* or *phrasal verbs*).

5 Think about whether you need to make a grammatical change (e.g. from active to passive) or a vocabulary change (e.g. change *escape* to the phrasal verb *get away*, or change a linking expression like *because* to *on account of*).

Tip! Check whether you need to make any other changes (e.g. a noun to an adjective, an affirmative to a negative).

6 Check you have included all the information from the first sentence and that you haven't added anything.

Tip! If you can't complete the whole answer, write what you can – you may get one mark.

7 Check that the completed sentence makes sense.

Tip! Check that your spelling is correct. You will lose marks for spelling mistakes.

Follow the exam instructions on page 48, using the advice to help you.

Tip! For some questions, more than one answer is possible. But you should only give one of them.

Tip! Check the number of words you've used. Remember that contracted forms (e.g. *I'm*) count as two words, except *can't* (= *cannot*) which counts as one.

For questions **35–42**, complete the second sentence so that it has a similar meaning to the first sentence, using the word given. **Do not change the word given.** You must use between **two** and **five** words, including the word given. Here is an example (**0**).

0 Maybe Carla didn't receive the email I sent her.

MAY

Carla .... the email I sent her.

The gap can be filled by the words 'may not have received', so you write:

Example: | 0 | MAY NOT HAVE RECEIVED |

Advice

0 You have to change the underlined words.

Negative past modal needed

1 mark for 'may not', 1 for 'have received'

35 Two verb forms are possible after 'remember'. Which is used when it refers to a past experience?

36 A modal form is needed here. Will it be positive or negative, present or past?

37 Be careful: 'worth' is not used with the same structure as 'point'.

38 Make sure you use the correct form of the irregular main verb.

39 You will need to form a phrasal verb and then use the correct form of the second verb.

40 Will this sentence need to be positive or negative? What verb form follows 'likely'?

41 Which phrasal verb means 'stop doing something'? Which verb form follows phrasal verbs?

42 A past modal form is needed. Which do we use when we're sure about something?

---

35 In 2009 I went to Shanghai and I will never forget it.
 REMEMBER
 I .... to Shanghai in 2009.

36 It was foolish of you to ride your bike so fast.
 SHOULD
 You .... your bike so fast.

37 There was no point in staying at the party because my friends had left.
 WORTH
 My friends had left the party so .... there.

38 It's possible that the thieves hid the money in the countryside.
 MIGHT
 The thieves .... the money in the countryside.

39 The climbers continued to go up the mountain even though it was snowing.
 CARRIED
 The climbers .... the mountain even though it was snowing.

40 There isn't much chance of the weather improving today.
 LIKELY
 The weather .... today.

41 I've decided that in future I'm not going to eat chocolate.
 GIVE
 I've decided that I'm going to .... chocolate.

42 I'm sure Luisa was very upset when she lost her money.
 HAVE
 Luisa .... very upset when she lost her money.

Test 1 Training — PAPER 4 Listening Part 1

Task information

- In Part 1 you hear eight short unrelated extracts from monologues or exchanges. There is one multiple choice question per extract, each with three options. You hear each extract twice.

- Part 1 tests your understanding of: gist, detail, opinion, attitude, function, purpose, relationship, topic, place, situation, agreement, etc.

- You can both read and listen to each question.

- The question includes information about the situation (e.g. a phone call, a radio programme, an extract from a play, etc.) followed by a direct question (e.g. *How does she feel?*).

Understanding distraction

1 Study this multiple-choice question and the recording script below. Why is B correct? Why are A and C wrong?

> 1 You hear a man talking about buying a bicycle. What most attracted him to this bike?
>
>   **A** its special features
>   **B** its condition
>   **C** its price

'I saw it advertised in the local newspaper and I thought I'd ring the seller to see if it was still for sale and <u>whether he'd drop the price because it seemed a bit high to me.</u> He wouldn't, but I liked the sound of it and we arranged a time for me to call round later. Well as soon as I saw it, I knew I had to have it. <u>It was just an ordinary bike really, nothing remarkable about it at all</u>, but <u>it'd obviously been very well looked after. It was a few years old, but you really couldn't tell.</u> So I bought it there and then.'

— C
— A
— B

Tip! Don't choose your answer until you've heard the whole text at least once.

2a 🎧02 Look at the next question and listen twice to the recording. Which is the correct answer, A, B or C? Why?

> 2 You overhear a conversation in a café between two young people. Why didn't she call him?
>
>   **A** She didn't have his number.
>   **B** It was too late in the evening.
>   **C** Her phone wasn't working.

b 🎧02 Listen again. Why are the other two answers wrong?

Tip! You won't hear the same words as the words in the question, so listen for the same idea.

Listening Part 1

Test 1 Exam practice — Listening Part 1

Action plan

1. For each question, quickly read the first line. What's the situation? Will you hear one person or two? Female or male?
2. Look at the direct question (e.g. *Who is the woman?*) and underline these words.
3. When you first hear the recording, try to think of an answer to each question in your own words. Then choose (from A, B or C) the option most like your answer.
4. Check your answer the second time you listen, making sure that you have not made a mistake – speakers may use words connected with more than one option.
5. If you're still not sure which is the correct answer, cross out any you are sure are wrong and guess.
6. When the recording has finished and you have chosen your answer, forget about that question and concentrate on the next one.

03 Follow the exam instructions on page 51, using the advice to help you.

Tip! Before you listen, think of other expressions for the words in the question, e.g. 'What does he do?' – *he works in …, his job is …, he's employed as …*, etc.

Tip! Make sure you always know which number text you are listening to.

You will hear people talking in eight different situations. For questions **1–8**, choose the best answer (**A**, **B** or **C**).

1 You hear a man talking about his work.
   What is his job?

   A journalist
   B office manager
   C salesman

2 You hear part of a radio discussion about a TV nature programme.
   What did the speaker find disappointing about it?

   A the quality of the photography
   B the choice of place to film in
   C the amount of information given

3 You hear a woman and a man talking.
   Who are they?

   A wife and husband
   B employer and employee
   C teacher and student

4 You hear two people talking about air pollution in the city.
   What do they agree about?

   A the effects of high population density in the city centre
   B the need to reduce the amount of traffic in the city centre
   C the amount of pollution caused by factories on the outskirts

5 You hear a woman talking on the phone to an airline.
   What is the purpose of her call?

   A to complain about something
   B to ask them for information
   C to ask them to do something

6 You hear a young man talking on a cellphone to a friend.
   Where does he want his friend to meet him?

   A inside the football stadium
   B at the railway station
   C at a café near the stadium

7 You switch on the radio in the middle of a programme.
   What kind of programme is it?

   A a quiz show
   B an interview
   C a news programme

8 You hear a woman talking about a camping holiday she went on as a teenager.
   How did she feel during the holiday?

   A annoyed by the behaviour of others
   B miserable because of the bad weather
   C disappointed with where they stayed

Advice

1 What does each of A–C do in their job? Where do they work?

2 The recording mentions camera work, the location and learning from the programme, but which of these does it describe negatively?

3 Which words might you expect to hear in a conversation in each of A–C?

4 At the beginning of each person's reply, listen for expressions that indicate agreement and disagreement.

5 Listen for an expression that's often used to complain, ask for information or ask someone to do something.

6 Be careful with changes of plan, and references to 'there'.

7 Does the man ask the kind of questions that produce 'right' or 'wrong' answers? Or are they talking about the woman's life? Or about current events?

8 Listen to the speaker's tone, as well as the words she uses. When does she sound unhappy: when she's talking about other people, the weather, or the place?

Listening Part 1

Test 1 Training — Listening Part 2

Task information

- In Part 2 you will hear a monologue or interacting speakers lasting approximately three minutes.
- Part 2 tests your understanding of detail, stated opinion and specific information.
- You have to listen for particular words, phrases or numbers to complete ten sentences. You should write these down exactly as you hear them.
- The 1–3 words you have to write will not be above First Certificate level.
- Sometimes words or names are spelt out. If so, you must spell them correctly.
- All the questions follow the order of the information in the recording, and for each one you will hear a 'cue' that indicates an answer is coming.

Tip! Be careful with words, phrases or numbers you hear which may *seem* to fit the gaps, but are not correct.

Thinking about possible answers; listening for cues

1 Study exam question 9 and the extract from the recording script below.
Why is *a child* correct in question 9? Would any other answer be possible?
What mistakes might a candidate listening to this make? Why?

Rabbits are not suitable pets for | *a child* | **9** | as they need a lot of care.

Tip! You may need to write three words, but often you need only write one or two.

Rabbits are clean, intelligent and friendly animals, and they make excellent pets. They do, though, require a considerable amount of attention in order to keep them healthy, comfortable and safe, so (9) it is better if an adult or a teenager, rather than a child, looks after them. As they are such sociable animals, preferring to live in pairs or groups, it is advisable to have at least two.

— cue (similar to *need a lot of care*)
— correct answer

2a 🎧 04 Look at question 10 below and listen twice to the extract from the same recording.

Inside the house, you should remove any | | **10** | to keep the rabbits safe.

b Write down the correct answer. Why is it correct?

c 🎧 04 Listen again. What is the cue? Which other phrase could be mistaken for the right answer?

Test 1 Exam practice — Listening Part 2

Action plan

1. Read the instructions to get an idea of the situation.
2. Quickly go through the incomplete sentences, including any words after the gaps.
3. For each gap, decide what kind of information (e.g. *object, number*) you need to listen for.
4. The first time you listen, write your answer in pencil, in case you want to change it on the second listening.
5. When the recording has finished, check the sentences all make sense – and check your spelling, too.

Tip! Underline the key words in each question, then listen for words and phrases that express the same idea.

05 Follow the exam instructions, using the advice to help you.

Tip! Before you listen, get an idea of what the text is about by quickly reading through all the sentences.

You will hear part of an interview with a man called Ewan Richardson, who is trying to persuade people to use less paper. For questions **9–18**, complete the sentences.

Every year, the average UK citizen uses about [**9**] of paper.

Most of the world's paper comes from very [**10**] forests.

The production of paper causes terrible [**11**] in some places.

The destruction of the forests is a much bigger cause of global warming than [**12**].

Ewan says that there are already paper recycling bins in many [**13**].

You can use less paper by avoiding unnecessary [**14**] when you are studying or working.

You can often reuse [**15**] that you have received.

To receive less junk mail, don't ask for [**16**] when you buy something.

Stop receiving any magazines you don't always read, or [**17**] them with others.

Most [**18**] published in Britain are now printed on recycled paper.

Advice

9 You will hear several different figures, but only one refers to 'the average UK citizen'.

10 Listen to everything the speaker says about this, not just his first sentence.

11 Keep listening after you've answered 10. The cue for 11 comes soon after.

12 Other causes are mentioned – but are they smaller, or bigger?

13 Listen for where the bins are 'already', not where they are planned for the future.

14 The cue is a different structure that also means 'use less'.

15 Which of the things mentioned can you actually 'reuse'?

16 How do firms who send junk mail get people's addresses?

17 What kind of word (e.g. noun, adjective) do you need here?

18 He mentions three kinds of publishing, but the statement is only true for one of them.

Test 1 Training Listening Part 3

Task information

- In Part 3 you hear five short related monologues.
- Part 3 tests your understanding of: gist, detail, opinion, attitude, function, purpose, relationship, topic, place, situation, agreement, etc.
- The instructions you see and hear include information about the link between the five recordings (e.g. the speakers are all talking about the weather, or they are all complaining about something).
- The questions do not usually follow the order of the information in the recording.

Dealing with distraction

1 Study this exam task and the recording script for Speaker 1 below. Why is C correct for question 19? Why are A and F wrong?

You will hear five different people talking about unfortunate events. For questions **19–23**, choose from the list (**A–F**) what each speaker says. Use the letters only once. There is one extra letter which you do not need to use.

A   having something stolen

B   falling over

C   arriving late for work

D   being hurt in an accident

E   failing a test

F   missing a train

Speaker 1   [C]   19

Speaker 2   [ ]   20

> <u>I kept looking at my watch and I realised I wasn't going to make it</u>. They'd told me that <u>if I didn't get in on time this morning, I'd have to look for another job</u>, so this was a disaster. But it was so unfair. I'd done everything right: I'd got up at 7.30, left the house at 8 and <u>caught the early train</u> into town. It was just my bad luck that it broke down as soon as it left the station. I thought of calling to explain what'd happened, but I couldn't find my phone and <u>at first I thought a thief must have taken it. Then I remembered that in my hurry to go out, I'd left it on the kitchen table</u>.

C

C

F

A

Tip! Before you answer a question, wait until you have heard everything the speaker has to say.

2a 🎧 06 Listen twice to Speaker 2 and answer question 20. Which is the correct answer, A, B, D, E or F? Which parts of the text tell you?

b 🎧 06 Listen again. Which two sentences might *seem* to be right, but are not? Why are they wrong?

Tip! Listen for ideas, not just individual words, that are similar to those in A–F.

Test 1 Exam practice — Listening Part 3

Action plan

1 Quickly read the instructions and sentences A–F. What is the link between the five recordings?
2 Study options A–F and underline the key words in each.
3 Before you listen, think of words or phrases that the speakers might use to talk about different aspects of the topic.
4 The first time you hear the recording, listen for the general idea of what each speaker says.
5 Choose the answer to each question that you think is right.
6 The second time you listen, check that each of A–F exactly matches what the speaker says.

🎧 07 Follow the exam instructions, using the advice to help you.

Tip! Be careful: speakers may mention something connected with more than one option, but there is only one correct answer.

You will hear five different young people talking about renting homes. For questions **19–23**, choose from the list (**A–F**) what each speaker says. Use the letters only once. There is one extra letter which you do not need to use.

A Something dangerous needed to be repaired.

Speaker 1 ☐ 19

B It was often cold indoors.

Speaker 2 ☐ 20

C There was a pleasant view from the window.

Speaker 3 ☐ 21

D The neighbours were very noisy.

Speaker 4 ☐ 22

E The rent was too high.

Speaker 5 ☐ 23

F The furniture was good quality.

Advice

A Don't choose the wrong answer because you hear the speaker mention something that was <u>not</u> a danger. Keep listening.

B Speakers 1, 2 & 5 all talk about cold conditions, but only one talks about it being cold indoors.

C Two speakers describe views, but which sounds 'pleasant'?

D Speakers 2, 3 & 5 all mention 'neighbours', but which of **them** made too much noise?

E What's another way of saying you were paying too much?

F Two speakers mention furniture, but was it 'good quality'?

Tip! When you have chosen an answer, cross it out lightly in pencil so that you can concentrate on the others.

Test 1 Training — Listening Part 4

Task information

- In Part 4 you will hear a monologue or interacting speakers lasting approximately three minutes. There are seven multiple choice questions each with three options.
- Part 4 tests your understanding of: attitude, opinion, gist, main ideas and specific information.
- All the questions follow the order of the information in the recording; each part of the recording relates to a particular question.
- The instructions you see and hear may include information such as the main speaker's name, occupation or hobby, and/or the setting (e.g. a radio interview). This can tell you the type of language and information you might hear.

Understanding distraction; listening for cues

1 Study this multiple-choice question and the extract from the recording script. It is from a radio interview in which Dave Harris asks Lucy Williams about her work as a police officer. Why is A correct? Why are B and C wrong?

1   How does Lucy feel about her work now?
   A She likes the fact that she never gets bored.
   B She dislikes having to deal with aggressive people.
   C She would prefer to work in an office.

Dave	So tell me, Lucy, <u>what have you found to be the positive things about police work? What's the negative side to it?</u> — *Cue*
Lucy	Well, I often come into contact with people who are upset or angry, maybe causing trouble, and I have to calm them down and in some cases make it clear I'm in authority. But <u>I just see that as part of the job, and in fact I'd probably miss it</u> if I were given <u>a desk job. I'd find that really dull</u> compared to being out on the street, which is <u>always interesting because no two days are ever the same. You never know what to expect next, and that's great.</u> — *B* / *C* / *A*

Tip! For every question you will hear a 'cue' – words that express a similar idea to the question – that tells you the answer is in that part of the recording.

Tip! The options use phrases or sentences that rephrase, summarise or report the ideas in the text.

2a 🎧 08 Look at the next question and listen twice to the extract from the same interview. Which is the correct answer, A, B or C? Why?

2   What advice does she give to teenagers?
   A join the police instead of going to university
   B begin by working part-time for the police
   C do a different job before joining the police

b 🎧 08 Listen again. What is the cue? Why are the other two answers wrong?

Test 1 Exam practice — Listening Part 4

Action plan

1 Quickly read the instructions. What kind of recording is it? What's the topic? Who will you hear?

2 Before you listen, look at the first line of each item. What kind of information, e.g. somebody's opinion, do you need for each?

3 Underline the key words in each item to help you focus on the information you need.

4 Listen for expressions with similar or opposite meanings to the key words you underlined.

5 Think of an answer in your own words. Then choose the option most like your answer.

6 Check all your answers on the second listening.

09 Follow the exam instructions, using the advice to help you.

Tip! After you hear the instructions, there's a one-minute pause before the recording begins. Use this to look through the questions, underlining the key words.

You will hear a radio interview with Louise Graham, who works as a group leader at Ravensfield Outdoor Adventure Centre. For questions **24–30**, choose the best answer (**A**, **B** or **C**).

24 How long has Louise been working at Ravensfield?
   A about six months
   B about one year
   C about two years

25 When she started working at the centre, she felt
   A a little afraid of being injured doing her job.
   B rather nervous in case she did her job badly.
   C more confident than she thought she would.

26 What does she most enjoy about working with children?
   A thinking of new things for them to do
   B helping the less able ones achieve more
   C ensuring that they behave well at all times

27 How does she feel about working at night?
   A It's a necessary part of the job.
   B It's unfair that she has to do it.
   C It's something that she enjoys.

28 At the end of a course, the children
   A get on much better with each other.
   B thank the staff for all they've done.
   C have gained useful qualifications.

29 An added advantage of working at Ravensfield is that
   A she has made some new friends.
   B she can now afford to run a car.
   C she has long summer holidays.

30 What does she want to do in the future?
   A work in a bigger centre
   B get promotion at Ravensfield
   C go into a different kind of work

Advice

24 What kind of information do you need to listen for?

25 Think of expressions with similar or opposite meanings to the adjectives 'afraid', 'nervous' and 'confident'.

26 She may enjoy two or even all three of these. Listen for a superlative adjective.

27 Decide what the focus of this question is. Which word tells you?

28 Listen only for what the **children** do.

29 Listen for whether she's talking about the present or the future.

30 Be careful with ideas that are mentioned, but then rejected. Which of A–C does she reject?

Test 1 Training — PAPER 5 Speaking Part 1

Task information

- Part 1 lasts about three minutes.
- One of the examiners tells you their names and asks for yours. Then you give him/her your mark sheet.
- You answer questions from one of the examiners.
- You don't usually talk to the other candidate.
- Part 1 tests your ability to give basic information about yourself and to talk about everyday topics such as your work or studies, your family, your free time and your future plans.
- One aim of Part 1 is to help you relax by getting you to talk about a topic you know a lot about: yourself.
- To find out how your speaking will be assessed, go to the Cambridge ESOL website: http://www.cambridgeesol.org/assets/pdf/resources/teacher/fce_hb_dec08.pdf, page 86.

Useful language: basic expressions

1 Write the expressions in the box next to the correct purpose.

> also   and often   as well as that   because
> ~~for example~~   for instance   like   Pardon?
> so   such as   the reason is
> Could you say that again, please?
> Sorry, I didn't catch that.

To give an example: *for example* ....

To give a reason: ....

To add information: ....

To ask for repetition: ....

2 🎧 10 You will hear two candidates, Hanif and Yara, doing Part 1. Read the examiner's questions, then listen and decide which of statements 1–6 are true. Write Yes or No for each person.

Examiner's questions
Where are you from?
What do you like about living there?
What sort of things do you do in your free time?
Which country would you most like to visit?
In what ways do you think you will use English?

		Hanif	Yara
1	sounds quite confident	No	......
2	is generally easy to understand	......	......
3	gives full answers to the questions	......	......
4	uses quite a wide range of language	......	......
5	is polite to the examiner	......	......
6	probably gets a good mark for Part 1	......	......

3 🎧 10 Listen again. Which of the expressions from Exercise 1 do they use?

Test 1 Exam practice — Speaking Part 1

Action plan

1 Be polite and friendly when you meet the examiners and the other candidate.
2 Listen carefully to the examiner's questions. If you don't understand something, politely ask him or her to repeat it (e.g. *Could you repeat that, please?*).
3 Don't just reply *yes* or *no* to the questions.
4 Don't try to give a speech or repeat sentences that you prepared earlier.
5 Make sure you speak loudly and clearly enough for the examiners and your partner to hear you. Be confident!
6 Where you can, give reasons and examples in your answers.
7 Try to use a wide range of grammar and vocabulary.

Tip! While you are speaking, look at the examiner who asks you the questions, not at the other candidate.

If you have a partner, answer these questions in pairs.

Part 1 3 minutes (5 minutes for groups of three)

Interlocutor First of all, we'd like to know something about you.

- Where are you from?

- What do you like about living there?

- What is your favourite place for a holiday?

- When do you like to listen to music?

- Do you enjoy playing computer games? Why?/Why not?

Tip! Listen to the examiner and your partner when they are speaking to each other. This will help you get used to their voices.

Test 1 Training — Speaking Part 2

Task information

- In Part 2, each candidate is given a one-minute 'long turn'. Nobody will interrupt you.
- The examiner gives each of you two pictures and will ask you to compare them, and answer a question which is written at the top of the page.
- This part tests your ability to organise your speaking, and to compare, describe and give your opinions.
- You also talk for 20 seconds about your partner's pictures, after their minute has finished.

Useful language: comparing and contrasting

1 Study pictures A and B on page C1, then write these headings above the correct groups of sentences (1–5).

> Guessing   Contrasting the pictures   Saying which you'd prefer to do
> Comparing the pictures   Saying which picture you're talking about

1 ....
   The picture at the top shows people doing an exercise class.
   In the second photo, there are some people playing tennis.
   In the one at the bottom, there's a match going on.
   They both show people taking part in sports.
   In both of them there are people doing sports.

2 ....
   He **seems/looks** a bit worried at the moment.
   He **looks as if** he's going to win the match.
   They **look like** professional tennis players
   They **might/may/could be** playing in an important final.
   Perhaps/Maybe it's been a very long match.
   It's **probably** going to finish soon.

3 ....
   I think the tennis players **are** fitt**er than** the people in the exercise class.
   Playing tennis like that is **more** excit**ing than** doing an exercise class.
   These people are moving much **more** quick**ly than** those people.

4 ....
   Tennis is a competitive sport, **but** an exercise class isn't.
   An exercise class is usually an indoor activity, **while** tennis is usually played outside.
   Those people are playing to win, **whereas** the others are doing it to get fit.
   They get paid for taking part. **On the other hand**, these people have to pay to do this.
   You need a proper court to play tennis. **In contrast,** you can do this kind of exercise anywhere.

5 ....
   I prefer to do exercise with lots of other people.
   I enjoy fast-moving sports **more than** slower activities.
   I'd rather do something non-competitive.
   I find racket sports **more** fun **than** doing the same exercise again and again.

2 You will hear Yara and Hanif talking about two pictures in Speaking Part 2. Read these instructions and the question above photos A and B on page C2. What *two* things does Yara (Candidate A) have to do? What does Hanif (Candidate B) have to do?

> **Part 2**   4 minutes (6 minutes for groups of three)
>
> *(Candidate A)*, it's your turn first. Here are your photographs on page C2. They show **young people with others who are close to them.**
>
> I'd like you to compare the photographs, and say **why the two different kinds of relationship are important to teenagers.** Talk about your photographs on your own for about a minute.
>
> *(Candidate B)*, **do you prefer to spend your free time with family or with friends?**

3a Look at the photos and think about the instructions. Which of these things do you think Yara should and shouldn't do? Put a ✔ or a ✘ next to 1–10. Give reasons for the things she *shouldn't* do.

   1 Say what each person in both pictures is wearing.
   2 Suggest who the different groups of people might be.
   3 Say what the two groups are doing at the moment.
   4 Contrast the ages of the people in the two pictures.
   5 Talk about what the people might do next.
   6 Give examples of the things young people can do with friends.
   7 Give reasons why young people need to have friends.
   8 Describe her own family and her closest friends.
   9 Give examples of the things young people do with their family.
  10 Say why young people sometimes need their family's support.

b 🎧11 Now listen to the recording and check whether Yara only talked about the things you ticked.

4 🎧11 Listen again. Tick ✔ the expressions similar to those in *Useful language* on page 60 that Yara and Hanif use. Which expressions does Yara use to introduce reasons and examples?

Speaking Part 2   Test 1 Training | 61

Test 1 Exam practice — Speaking Part 2

Action plan

1 Listen to the instructions, study the pictures and read the question.

2 Think about what you're going to say.

Tip! Imagine you're describing the pictures to somebody who can't see them.

3 Don't speak *too* quickly, or for less than a minute. The examiner will say when it's time to stop.

4 Don't try to describe every detail. Just say what's similar and different about the pictures.

5 If you can't name something you can see, use other words to explain (e.g. *the thing you use for ...*).

6 When you answer the examiner's question, give your opinion, with reasons and possibly examples.

Tip! Make sure you spend enough time on both comparing the photos and answering the question about them.

7 Never interrupt your partner in Part 2. Listen and think about what they say, so you can comment afterwards when the examiner asks you a question.

---

1 Look at the exam instructions below and photos A and B on page C3.

1 What two things do you (Candidate A) have to do?
2 What does your partner (Candidate B) have to do?
3 What will you say about the pictures?
4 How will you answer the question above the pictures?

2 If you have a partner, do this exam task in pairs.

Tip! If you make a mistake, it's fine to correct yourself, but it's also important to keep talking and complete the task.

(Candidate A), it's your turn first. Here are your photographs on page C3. They **show people having fun.**

I'd like you to compare the photographs, and say **what you think could be exciting about doing these things.**

(Candidate B), **which of these would you rather do?**

---

3 Look at the exam instructions below and photos A and B on page C4.

1 What two things does your partner (Candidate B) have to do?
2 What do you (Candidate A) have to do?
3 What could your partner say to compare and contrast the pictures?
4 How do you think he or she will answer the question above the pictures?
5 How will you answer the question the examiner asks you (Candidate A)?

4 If you have a partner, do this exam task in pairs.

Tip! Before the exam, gets lots of practice talking about pictures. A minute can seem a long time!

Now, *(Candidate B)*, here are your photographs on page C4. **They show people creating images of wildlife.**

I'd like you to compare the photographs, and say **why you think the activity is important to the different people.**

(Candidate A), **do you prefer to paint/draw what you see, or take photos?**

Test 1 Training — Speaking Part 3

Task information

- Part 3 lasts about three or four minutes. You work in pairs.
- The examiner gives you a piece of paper with one or more pictures that show different ideas or possibilities, and tells you what you have to do.
- First you talk about the pictures together, giving your opinions. Then you try to make a decision.
- This part tests your ability to talk about different possibilities, make suggestions, express opinions and give reasons, agree or disagree, and attempt to decide together.
- You take turns so that your partner and you spend about the same amount of time speaking.

Useful language: suggestions

Complete the headings above each group of expressions (1–5) with these words.

| Agreeing with   Asking if someone agrees with |
| Disagreeing politely with |
| Giving reasons for disagreeing with   Making |

1 .... suggestions
   How about ...?
   Why don't we ...?
   Perhaps we should ...?
   What do you think ...?
   So shall we ..., then?

2 .... suggestions
   Don't you think so?
   Would you agree?
   Wouldn't you say so?
   Is that all right with you?
   Would you go along with that?

3 .... suggestions
   Right.
   I think so, too.
   That's true.
   I completely agree with you.
   That's a great idea.

4 .... suggestions
   I'm not really sure about that.
   I think it might be better to ...
   I think I'd rather ...
   I don't really agree. I think ...
   I'm not so keen on ...

5 .... suggestions
   That's because ...
   For one thing, ... (for another ...)
   Well, the thing is ...
   I think the problem is that ...
   The main reason is that ...

Focusing on instructions and pictures; listening for expressions

1 Look at the exam instructions below and the pictures on page C5.
   1 What is the topic of the discussion?
   2 What two things do you have to do?
   3 How many objects are there? What are they?

> **Part 3**   3 minutes (4 minutes for groups of three)
>
> Now, I'd like you to talk about something together for about three (four) minutes.
>
> **Here are some things that you often find in the home.**
>
> *Show candidates pictures on page C5.*
>
> First, talk to each other about how useful these things are to the family. Then decide which two things are most important to you.

2 🎧 12 Listen to two candidates, Marisol and Han, doing this task and answer questions 1–7 with *Yes* or *No*.
   1 Do they listen and reply to each other?   Yes
   2 Do they use polite expressions when they disagree?   ....
   3 Do they give reasons and examples?   ....
   4 Do they spend some time discussing each picture?   ....
   5 Do they take turns and talk for about the same time?   ....
   6 Do they try to decide on which objects to choose?   ....
   7 Do they agree on a choice of objects? If so, which?   ....

3 🎧 12 Listen again and tick ✔ the expressions similar to the *Useful language* on the left.

Test 1 Exam practice / Speaking Part 3

Action plan

1 Listen carefully to the instructions and look at the pictures with your partner.

Tip! If you need to check the instructions while you are doing the task, you can read them at the top of the page.

2 Start the discussion with something like *Would you like to start, or shall I?* or *Shall we begin with this one?*

3 Begin by talking about one of the pictures, giving your opinion, or perhaps making a suggestion. Then ask what your partner thinks, and why.

4 Talk briefly about each picture. Reply to your partner's ideas and give reasons for your suggestions, opinions and preferences. If you disagree with him or her, be polite.

5 Bring the discussion towards a conclusion by saying, for example, *So which do you think would be best?* or *Which shall we go for, then?*

6 Try to decide which to choose (e.g. *Shall we do this one?* or *I'm in favour of that one*).

7 If you agree, say something like *Right, that's what we'll do.* If you can't decide, you can say *Shall we leave it at that, then?* or simply *Let's agree to disagree.*

Tip! Don't try to reach a decision too quickly – three minutes is quite a long time when you're talking.

---

1 Study the exam instructions below and the pictures on pages C6–C7.

   1 What do you have to imagine?
   2 What two things do you have to do?
   3 How many suggestions are there and what is each called?

2 If you have a partner, do this exam task in pairs.

Tip! Keep the conversation moving, for instance by saying *What do you think of this idea?* or *Let's look at the next one.*

Part 3

Interlocutor   Now, I'd like you to talk about something together for about three minutes. *(4 minutes for groups of three)*

   I'd like you to imagine that your town or village wants to hold an open-air concert as part of its summer festival. Here are some pictures of the suggestions they are considering.

Show candidates pictures on pages C6–C7.

   First, talk to each other about which kinds of music would be popular with people in general. Then decide which two kinds young people would enjoy most.

Tip! Don't speak for a long time without letting your partner say anything. You may lose marks if you don't take turns.

Test 1 Training — Speaking Part 4

Task information

- Part 4 lasts about four minutes. You both answer questions based on the same topic as Part 3.
- This part tests your ability to talk about issues in more depth than in the other three parts of the Speaking paper. You will need to express opinions and give reasons for them, and also to agree or disagree with different opinions.
- The examiner may also ask you to reply to your partner's opinions.
- You may want to bring your partner into the discussion, and they might want to involve you in answering their questions, too.
- After you finish Part 4, the examiner will thank you and say the test has ended.

Useful language: opinions

Complete the expressions with these words. In some cases, more than one answer is possible, and you can use some words more than once.

feel	feeling	feelings	hand
might	opinion	possible	say
seems	think	views	way

Asking for someone's opinion
1 What's your __opinion__ of ...?
2 What do you _____ about ...?
3 What are your _____ about ...?
4 How do you _____ about ...?
5 Could you tell me your _____ on ...?

Giving your opinion
6 I _____ ...
7 I'd _____ that ...
8 it _____ to me ...
9 in my _____ ...
10 my own _____ is that ...

Trying to change someone's opinion
11 yes, but isn't it _____ that ...?
12 yes, but on the other _____
13 but don't you _____ that ...?
14 well, others _____ say ...
15 another _____ of looking at it would be ...

Predicting points; listening for expressions

1 Think about the topic of Part 3 (things in the home). Which of points 1–6 do you think the examiner might ask you to discuss? Put a ✔ or a ✘ next to each point. Why are the others unlikely in Part 4?

1 whether houses are too expensive to buy
2 whether everyone in a house should do the same amount of housework
3 how common electrical appliances work
4 whether homes have too much electrical equipment
5 whether you enjoy doing housework
6 which electrical things you have in your house

2 🎧 13 You will hear Han and Marisol doing Part 4. Decide which of 1–6 is true (T) or false (F) for each person.

		Han	Marisol
1	asks the examiner to repeat the question	F	......
2	asks for their partner's opinion	......	......
3	gives reasons for their opinions	......	......
4	gives examples to support their opinions	......	......
5	tries to change their partner's opinion	......	......
6	is polite to the examiner and their partner	......	......

3 🎧 13 Listen again. Tick ✔ the expressions similar to the *Useful language* on the left that Han, Marisol and the examiner use.

Test 1 Exam practice — Speaking Part 4

Action plan

1 Part 4 questions are not written down, so listen carefully. If you don't understand something, ask the examiner to repeat it (e.g. *I'm sorry, I didn't catch the last word*).

2 Justify your opinions by giving reasons and possibly an example beginning *for instance, for example* or *such as ...* .

3 Avoid answers like 'I don't know'. If you don't know a lot about the subject, say so and give your opinion (e.g. *I don't know much about that, but I think ...*).

4 Listen carefully to what your partner says, possibly adding to their ideas.

5 Take turns and speak for about the same length of time. If you disagree with your partner's opinions, be polite.

6 Encourage your partner to say more (e.g. *How do you feel about that?* or *What would you do in that situation?*). Then reply.

Tip! Listen to everything that your partner says and show you are interested in the points that he or she makes.

7 When this part has ended, the Speaking test is over. Remember that the examiners can't answer questions about how well you did.

---

1 Think about the topic of Part 3 (the open-air concert). What issues do you think the examiner might ask you to discuss?

Tip! Look at the examiner when you are answering his or her questions, but at the other candidate when you are talking together.

2 Work in a group of three if possible. Decide who will be the 'examiner' and who will be the 'candidates'. The examiner should ask the candidates these questions:

Part 4

Interlocutor

- What else would you like to see at a summer festival? Why?

- How important in your life is music? Why?

- What do you think pop music will be like ten years from now?

Tip! Each time the examiner asks you a question, try to think of two or three things to say to answer it.

Test 2 Exam practice — PAPER 1 Reading Part 1

◄ **Page 10** *Task information*
◄ **Page 11** *Action plan*

1 Look at the exam instructions below. What kind of text (e.g. *magazine article*) is it?

Tip! Look at A–D *after* you read what the text says. Otherwise you may be misled by the wrong answers.

2 Read the text quickly.
1 Where is it set?
2 Who are the two people? Why are they there?
3 What are the main events in the extract?

3 Follow the exam instructions, using the advice to help you.

You are going to read an extract from a novel. For questions **1–8** on page 68, choose the answer (**A**, **B**, **C** or **D**) which you think fits best according to the text.

The sun was shining and Clare felt like doing something active. She'd had enough for the moment of living in the past. What she really wanted was some skiing if she could get herself organised. She walked into the ski school office and within ten minutes had arranged a private class for the whole afternoon. One of the ski teachers would meet her at the ski lift station at the end of the village at midday. The ski hire shop next door rented her some skis and boots and she carried them back to the hotel. There she changed into some more or less suitable clothes and took the hotel's electric taxi down to the lift station. She was a bit early and had time to look around, and get nervous. She hadn't skied for about ten years, though she'd been quite good at that time. Everyone said it was like riding a bike – you didn't forget how to do it. She stood there looking up at the mountains, trying to remember what to do.

'Madame Newton?'

'Yes,' she said. And there was her ski teacher, looking exactly like all the other ski teachers she remembered – sun-tanned and totally self-confident.

Half an hour later all thoughts of Ulrich Grunwalder and Edward Crowe had disappeared as she skied behind Bruno and concentrated on staying on her feet.

'Upper body still, make your legs do the work, Madame,' shouted Bruno over his shoulder.

'Call me Clare, please,' she said.

'OK. Lean forward a bit more, Clare. That's it. Good. You are remembering now, eh?'

'Yeah, I am … slowly. It's great. I'd forgotten what an amazing buzz skiing gives you.' They skied down some different runs with Bruno being wonderfully encouraging, and she really did begin to feel confident on the skis. Going up in the lifts, Clare and Bruno chatted – just the usual 'where are you from, what do you do' sort of chat, but it was pleasantly relaxing. In the middle of the afternoon, they stopped at an old farmhouse for coffee and apple cake. There were lots of other skiers, some of them also chatting with their teachers, doing the same. Clare felt as if she belonged – something about being part of a group, all with a shared interest, she supposed. It was a pleasant feeling she'd not had for a long time.

Bruno said hello to a few people, and went over to talk to one of the waiters. Clare took the opportunity to study him a little. Up until now, she'd just been skiing behind a man in a red ski suit, so it was interesting to see that he was quite tall, with curly brown hair and eyes to match. From the colour of his face he looked as if he'd spent his whole life in the open air. She guessed he was about forty.

'Are you in Zermatt long, Clare?' asked Bruno, after he'd been sitting with her a few minutes.

'Only a few days, probably. Just a short break to get away from everything at home,' replied Clare. She didn't feel like explaining the real reason. People looked at her differently when they knew. 'But I'd like to do some more skiing. Would you be able to do anything tomorrow?'

'I think so. But you'll have to book it through the Ski School office. I can't arrange anything with you directly,' said Bruno, putting on his gloves and standing up. 'Come on. Let's do a bit more now.'

'Great,' replied Clare.

After another hour, Clare said, 'Time to stop, I think.'

Bruno agreed. 'You should have a sauna tonight. It'll help your body relax. Not so stiff tomorrow, you know.'

Clare didn't care how stiff she was going to be tomorrow. She hadn't felt quite as good as this for months – full of fresh air, physically tired but in her mind – alive. Happy! Yes, that was how she felt!

Tip! Underline the key words in the stem. Then look for expressions in the text that mean the same or the opposite.

1 At the ski lift station, Clare felt nervous because
   A it was a long time since she had last gone skiing.
   B the ski instructor was late arriving for her lesson.
   C she was not appropriately dressed for skiing.
   D she had never really learnt how to ski properly.

2 After she had been skiing for 30 minutes, Clare
   A couldn't stop thinking about two other people.
   B got angry because Bruno was shouting at her.
   C asked Bruno to address her less formally.
   D knew she was in no danger of falling over.

3 What is meant by 'an amazing buzz' in line 31?
   A an interesting topic of conversation
   B a low, continuous sound
   C a sudden memory from long ago
   D a strong feeling of excitement

4 What does 'the same' refer to in line 40?
   A talking to ski instructors
   B having something to eat and drink
   C skiing on a number of slopes
   D taking ski lifts to the top of the slopes

5 What did Clare find enjoyable at the farmhouse?
   A being with people she hadn't met for a long time
   B talking to someone all the time she was there
   C having something in common with other people
   D thinking about the waiter's appearance and age

6 Why did Clare tell Bruno that she was there on holiday?
   A She wanted a different ski instructor the next day.
   B She thought he might react negatively to the truth.
   C She didn't want him to know she was leaving soon.
   D She felt that he was looking at her rather strangely.

7 How did Clare feel when they finished skiing for the day?
   A interested only in how she was at that time
   B delighted to find out how good a skier she was
   C sure that she would not be stiff the next day
   D keen to start skiing again immediately

8 What does Clare succeed in doing during this extract?
   A She thinks of a solution to the problem that brought her to Zermatt.
   B She talks to somebody else about her problems for the first time.
   C She realises that other people have similar problems to hers.
   D She discovers a way of taking her mind off her problems.

Advice

1 Quickly find the part of the first paragraph that mentions she was nervous, and study it carefully.

2 Look for an expression that means 'after 30 minutes' to find out what happened.

3 This tests your ability to work out meaning from context. What does 'it's great' tell you?

4 This tests your ability to find links within the text. Here, 'doing the same' is a way of avoiding repeating words. Which words?

5 Be careful with the location. She found chatting with Bruno 'pleasantly relaxing', but did this take place at the farmhouse?

6 What does she say about the reactions of people in general? Can we assume this includes Bruno?

7 What does she say about her feelings in the last paragraph? What was most important to her?

8 Think about the whole text. What is bothering her at the beginning? How does she deal with this?

Test 2 Exam practice / Reading Part 2

◂ Page 14 *Task information*
◂ Page 15 *Action plan*

1 Look at the exam instructions, the title and the introduction to the text in *italics* on page 70. What kind of text (e.g. *fiction, advertisement*) is it?

2 Follow the exam instructions, using the advice to help you.

Tip! Underline reference and linking expressions, vocabulary links and words that avoid repetition in both the main text and sentences A–H.

Tip! After you fill in all the gaps, read through the completed text. Can you see the links in ideas and language between the sentences from A–H and the main text?

A	Two young girls approached, nervously, to ask for a photograph.	E	When I get into the pool I'm very different to how I am outside it.
B	Those will help me improve my technique, and I can get even stronger because I'm still young.	F	With swimming in general, people don't recognise the amount of work that's needed.
C	Nowadays, though, they are hidden away somewhere safe.	G	It just means I don't need my parents to help me out.
D	That, however, was still slower than friend and team-mate Jo Jackson.	H	Particularly when you're not fully fit.

Tip! Each time you choose one of A–H, cross it out so that you don't have to keep reading through the whole list. This will save you time.

You are going to read part of an article in which a woman talks about her life after winning Olympic gold medals for swimming. Seven sentences have been removed from the article. Choose from the sentences **A–H** on page 69 the one which fits each gap (**9–15**). There is one extra sentence which you do not need to use.

Rebecca Adlington: top swimmer

Richard Wilson speaks to double Olympic champion Rebecca Adlington

When Rebecca Adlington won gold medals in the 400 metre and 800 metre freestyle events in Beijing, her life changed. It suddenly felt as though she inhabited two worlds: the one the public knew, the one they didn't know.

Last March she took part in the national championships, her first swimming competition since the Olympics. In the 800 metres she won in 8 minutes 18.86 seconds, four seconds outside the world record she set in Beijing, but still a time that only three women have ever bettered. Then, in the 400 metres, she broke the world record. **9** When she stood at the side of the pool and the television reporters asked if her victories at the Olympics had reduced her will to win, tears came into her eyes. But she held them back, because she had cried them already, in private.

'It was hard after the Olympics, with everybody expecting me to break a world record every time I got in the water,' she says. 'I was trying to handle that. Going into the national championships I wouldn't say I dealt with it particularly well. I was coming out of training sessions crying, because it's hard to live up to expectations. **10** Your mind plays tricks on you. I knew what I was doing in training before the Olympics; so going into something when I knew I wasn't doing those times is about trying to keep your confidence up. I needed to get away from it all and think about myself.'

By early the next year, with her standard not as it should have been, she started to say: no, I can't keep doing everything. 'I had to turn a lot of things down,' she admits, with a sigh. '**11** We do 90% training and 10% is the race. It's extremely demanding. After two hours of solid practice you're going to be pretty tired, and you have that in the morning and the evening, as well as gym.'

I spoke to her in the lobby of a hotel, where she seemed to be trying to make sense of it all. Her eyes are kind and friendly, and she always seems about to smile. She leans forward, attentive, as though there is nothing but you and her, at this moment. **12** She touched her blonde hair and happily let them take one.

Afterwards I ask how often people recognise her. 'It's mainly in the supermarket, or somewhere like that,' she laughs. She used to carry her two Olympic medals with her everywhere, ready to show them off when asked to. **13** In a place she knows they will always be there for her, and she is moving on.

Some things are no longer quite the same. After Beijing, she is under less financial pressure, as the amount of financial support she receives has doubled. Life is different, although not hugely. '**14** It's not that I'm rolling around in money, or that I can buy a Ferrari – I wish I could. It's a bit more freedom, that's all.'

Bill Furniss, her coach, describes how such a warm, bright and cheerful person changes to someone cold, focused and determined when she's competing. 'Yes,' she says, smiling. 'It's strange. **15** I don't know why. I want to be the best, to improve, to get faster.'

Advice

9 Negative reactions to breaking the world record seem surprising. Which sentence explains these, using a contrast link?

10 Which sentence mentions an extra difficulty she faced?

11 In which sentence does she talk about how much training she has to do?

12 Look for a noun that often forms a collocation with 'take', and the people referred to as 'them'.

13 Look for a contrast with 'used to', a reference word used instead of 'two Olympic medals', and a vocabulary contrast with 'show … off'.

14 Look for a sentence that suggests she is now better off financially, though not rich.

15 Which sentence describes a change in her personality?

Test 2 Exam practice — Reading Part 3

◀ **Page 17** *Task information*
◀ **Page 18** *Action plan*

1 Look at the exam instructions below and the title and layout of the text on page 72.
   1 What kind of text is it? How many parts is it in?
   2 What is the topic? Who are the people?
   3 What kind of information must you find?

2 Follow the exam instructions, using the advice to help you.

Tip! Remember that you may be able to choose two options A–D for some questions. In those cases, there are two spaces following the question.

You are going to read an article in which four young people say how they deal with the everyday stress in their lives. For questions **16–30**, choose from the people (**A–D**) on page 72. The people may be chosen more than once. When more than one answer is required, these may be given in any order.

Which person

regularly does a job without getting paid?	16	
no longer agrees to do things they don't want to do?	17	
tries to see the funny side of things that are worrying them?	18	
accepts that they sometimes make mistakes?	19	
is disappointed they can't see a particular kind of entertainment?	20	
prefers to do unpleasant jobs as soon as possible?	21	
is not doing as well in their studies as they would like?	22	
now enjoys doing something which they used to dislike?	23 / 24	
likes to tell friends about their problems?	25	
goes to bed quite early nowadays?	26	
sometimes breaks their own rules about eating when they are not alone?	27	
finds that acting makes them feel better?	28	
likes to think back to times when they felt less stressed?	29	
believes in putting off certain tasks?	30	

Advice

16 Look for another expression that means 'a job without getting paid'.

17 The expression 'no longer' indicates a change. What do people say if they don't agree to do something?

18 Think of a word associated with 'funny', but be careful that the context is correct.

19 Look for an expression which means anybody can make mistakes.

20 Find a complaint about the quality of one kind of entertainment.

21 Think of expressions with similar meanings to 'as soon as possible' and 'unpleasant'.

22 What does somebody who isn't doing well enough at school need to do?

Tip! When you are reading the text to find evidence, look for the same meanings as the questions, not the same words.

Tip! Remember that there may be parts of the text that are not tested.

Beating stress

A

School student **Ester Montoya** knows she has to improve her marks in her main subjects. She's trying hard, but it's not easy and sometimes she feels she's doing too much work. 'I have to get away from it now and then,' she says, 'so recently I've joined a local youth theatre group. It really helps because it takes my mind off everything, it's a kind of escape from reality. Also I'm meeting other people of my own age and I'm hoping to make some friends there. Apart from that I suppose there's TV, but there's not a lot on. I've read that laughing can be very relaxing, but I'm afraid none of the comedy series they're showing right now is worth watching. Something I've been meaning to try, though, is work helping others, perhaps old people. A friend of mine does it, and she says it really makes a difference – both to them and to her.'

B

For seventeen-year-old **Steve Ellison**, life is particularly busy right now. He's revising for some important exams but he still manages to find time for his favourite free-time activities, which include long-distance running. 'It's funny,' he says, 'I only took to it recently when I found it helped me wind down, because at school I never looked forward to those cross-country runs we had to do every Monday morning. Yet nowadays I run a lot at weekends, and I do some voluntary work with local kids at the sports centre.' As well as doing plenty of exercise, he also tries to maintain a healthy diet. 'I've told myself I must always eat a variety of healthy food, with lots of fruit and green vegetables, though if I'm out with my mates I may give in to temptation and have a burger and chips. I never drink coffee, though, because it makes you talk and act nervously, and it keeps you awake at night, too, which is bad for your stress level.'

C

First-year university student **Amelie Lefevre** believes that the best way to beat stress is to organise your life more sensibly. 'My life used to be pretty chaotic, there always seemed to be so much to do, often jobs that other people should have been doing. So what I eventually learned to do was to say *no*, politely, to extra work. That helped, as did making a list of priorities for each day, with some things scheduled for today, others for tomorrow and some that could be postponed for longer. I also make rules for myself about meal times, and the amount of sleep I need. There was a time when I was staying up until all hours, but I was exhausted the next day so I don't do that any more. I think I manage my time quite well now, but nobody's perfect and occasionally I still oversleep and turn up late for lectures!'

D

Student **Ndali Traore** likes to get up early so he has a relaxed start to the day. 'I hate leaving jobs till the last minute, and I always try to do those I like least first,' he says. 'These days I always listen to music while I'm working,' he adds, 'whereas a couple of years ago I found it annoying – it always seemed to spoil my concentration.' When he has some free time, he goes to the cinema, or out with friends. 'If something's bothering me,' he says, 'I often find that just talking to them about it helps. Particularly if you can make a joke about it, because it always seems a lot less serious when you do that.' If he's on his own, he has a special way of dealing with stress: 'I try to relive occasions when I was really relaxed, such as spending the day by a beautiful lake in the sunshine. That often works,' he says.

Test 2 Training — PAPER 2 Writing Part 1

> Page 20 *Task information*

Understanding the task; formal & informal language

1 Fill in the gaps in this text about Writing Part 1, using each item from the box once.

each	ending	formal	informal	own
paragraphs	plan	variety	120	150

In Writing Part 1, you read a letter or email with handwritten notes on it, then write a reply of between **(1)** ..... and **(2)** ..... words. Start with an appropriate introduction, organise the main part of your text into **(3)** ..... , and finish with a suitable **(4)** ..... . You should use the correct style, so to reply to an email from a friend, for example, you can use **(5)** ..... expressions, while a letter to someone like a College Director needs more **(6)** ..... language. Be careful with grammar, spelling and punctuation, and try to use a wide **(7)** ..... of words, phrases and structures. Always make a **(8)** ..... for your text before you start writing, listing the points you are going to mention about **(9)** ..... of the handwritten notes. Where possible, use your **(10)** ..... words rather than copying expressions from the text, but remember that you must include **all** the information you are asked for, or you will lose marks.

2 If you have a partner, work in pairs. Think of as many differences between formal and informal letters as you can (e.g. *longer words are usually formal, shorter words informal*).

3a With your partner, if you have one, think of four expressions for each of 1–6.
1 Requesting information
2 Expressing enthusiasm
3 Apologising
4 Expressing surprise
5 Advising
6 Changing the subject

b Which expressions are formal, and which are informal?

4a Look at this letter from Ms Helen Ryan, director of a summer camp for young people.

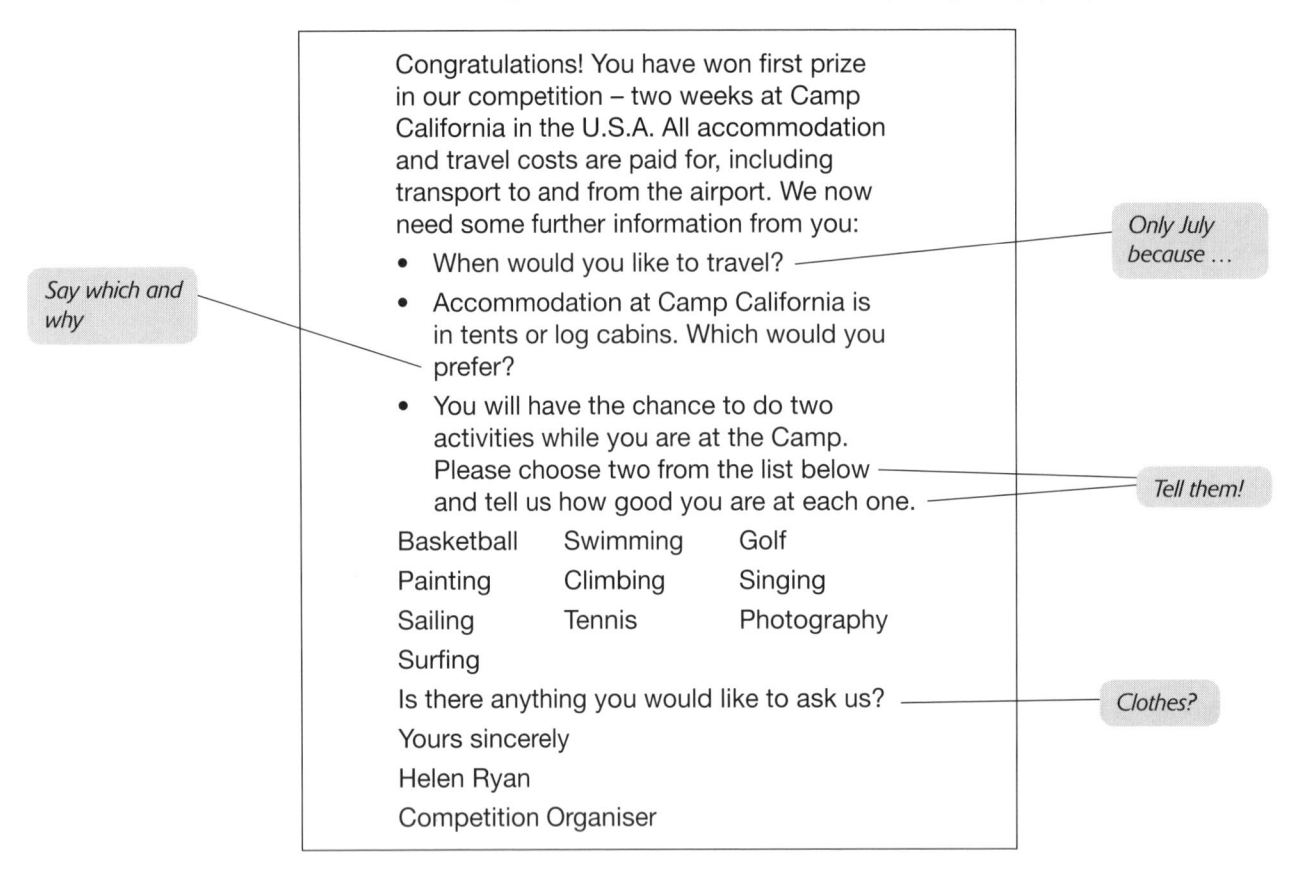

> Congratulations! You have won first prize in our competition – two weeks at Camp California in the U.S.A. All accommodation and travel costs are paid for, including transport to and from the airport. We now need some further information from you:
> - When would you like to travel?
> - Accommodation at Camp California is in tents or log cabins. Which would you prefer?
> - You will have the chance to do two activities while you are at the Camp. Please choose two from the list below and tell us how good you are at each one.
>
> Basketball   Swimming   Golf
> Painting   Climbing   Singing
> Sailing   Tennis   Photography
> Surfing
>
> Is there anything you would like to ask us?
> Yours sincerely
> Helen Ryan
> Competition Organiser

Annotations:
- When would you like to travel? → *Only July because …*
- Which would you prefer? → *Say which and why*
- tell us how good you are at each one. → *Tell them!*
- Is there anything you would like to ask us? → *Clothes?*

b Now read the letter below which was written by a First Certificate candidate in reply to Ms Ryan's letter. Stefan's letter is good, but the underlined expressions are too informal. Replace them with more suitable expressions.

> Dear Ms <u>Helen Ryan</u>,
>
> <u>Thanks a lot</u> for your <u>nice</u> letter. <u>I'm</u> very pleased to give you the information required.
>
> Firstly, the most suitable month for me would be July because <u>I'm</u> very busy with my studies <u>right now</u>, and <u>that's</u> when my holidays are.
>
> Secondly, <u>I'd</u> prefer to stay in a log cabin, because they are more comfortable. I confess that I have never been in a tent and <u>till</u> now I have never had any intention of doing so!
>
> The activities sound really interesting and <u>I'd</u> like to take part in some painting and climbing. Climbing<u>'s</u> an interesting activity where you need concentration, and <u>you're</u> working with your whole body. I <u>don't want to disappoint you</u>, but I am a beginner!
>
> <u>I'd appreciate it</u> if you could give me <u>a couple of</u> ideas about the clothes <u>I'll</u> need there.
>
> <u>Looking</u> forward to hearing from you.
>
> <u>Love</u>,
>
> Stefan Liakos

74 | Test 2 Training   Writing Part 1

Test 2 Exam practice — Writing Part 1

Page 23 *Action plan*

1 Look at the exam instructions below.
1. What do you have to imagine?
2. What kind of text (e.g. *email*) have you received?
3. Who wrote it? What is her job?
4. What do you have to do?

2 Look at the letter from Clara Romero. Is her letter written in an informal or formal style? Give some examples.

3 Do the exam task.

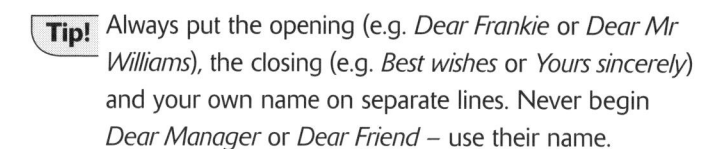

Tip! Always put the opening (e.g. *Dear Frankie* or *Dear Mr Williams*), the closing (e.g. *Best wishes* or *Yours sincerely*) and your own name on separate lines. Never begin *Dear Manager* or *Dear Friend* – use their name.

Tip! Use expressions such as *firstly* and *besides* to link points together to form a complete text.

Tip! When you've finished, make sure you've dealt with all the notes and have given appropriate answers. And don't forget to allow time to check your letter for mistakes.

You **must** answer this question. Write your answer in **120–150** words in an appropriate style.

You are helping to organise a trip abroad for a group of students who want to go to an international sports event. You have received a letter from Clara Romero, the director of the event. Read the letter and the notes you have made. Then write a letter to Ms Romero, using **all** your notes.

I am delighted to hear that your group will be able to attend. Which sports do they wish to take part in? — *Give details*

The event begins on the Saturday morning and will end quite early on the Sunday evening, which we hope will help everyone with their travel arrangements home. — *Yes, important to us because ...*

We can provide accommodation for your group on both the Friday and the Saturday night, or you can make your own arrangements. Please inform me of your preference. — *Say which and why*

If you would like further information, please do contact me. — *Ask for email and phone details*

Yours sincerely,
Clara Romero

Write your **letter**. You must use grammatically correct sentences with accurate spelling and punctuation in a style appropriate for the situation.

Test 2 Training — Writing Part 2 (report)

Page 24 *Writing Part 2 information*

Task information (report)

- The report task tests your ability to give factual information and make recommendations or suggestions.
- The instructions include a description of a situation. You have to write a report of between 120 and 180 words. Allow about 40 minutes for this task, including time at the end to check your work.
- The report may be for a teacher or school director, or classmates, members of the same club, etc. You therefore have to write in an appropriate style.
- Organise your text into report format and use headings if needed.
- Write full sentences and try to use correct grammar and punctuation, with a good range of language with accurate spelling.

Useful language: report

Put these expressions under the correct headings. Can you think of more to add under each heading?

It has been suggested that …	It would appear that …	To sum up, …	
It is felt that …	This report looks at …	The purpose of this report is to …	
It is said to be …	There would seem to be …	I would recommend that …	
In conclusion, …	I believe we should …	The aim of this report is to …	
I strongly recommend …	I (would) suggest …	This report is intended to show that …	

Introduction	Description and findings	Recommendations and suggestions	Conclusion
………………………	………………………	………………………	………………………
………………………	………………………	………………………	………………………
………………………	………………………	………………………	………………………
………………………	………………………	………………………	………………………
………………………	………………………	………………………	………………………

Understanding instructions

1 Study the exam instructions below and underline the key words.

1. What is the situation?
2. Who must you write a report for? Should the style be formal, informal or neutral (neither particularly formal nor informal)?
3. What two things do the instructions say you *must* do?
4. What else *should* you write, do you think?

> You have had a class discussion about sports and your teacher has asked you to suggest a sport that could be played at your college. Describe a sport that you have tried and say why you think it would be popular with students.
>
> Write your **report**.

2 ⊙ The answer below was written by Tomasz, a First Certificate candidate. Quickly read his report and think of a title for it.

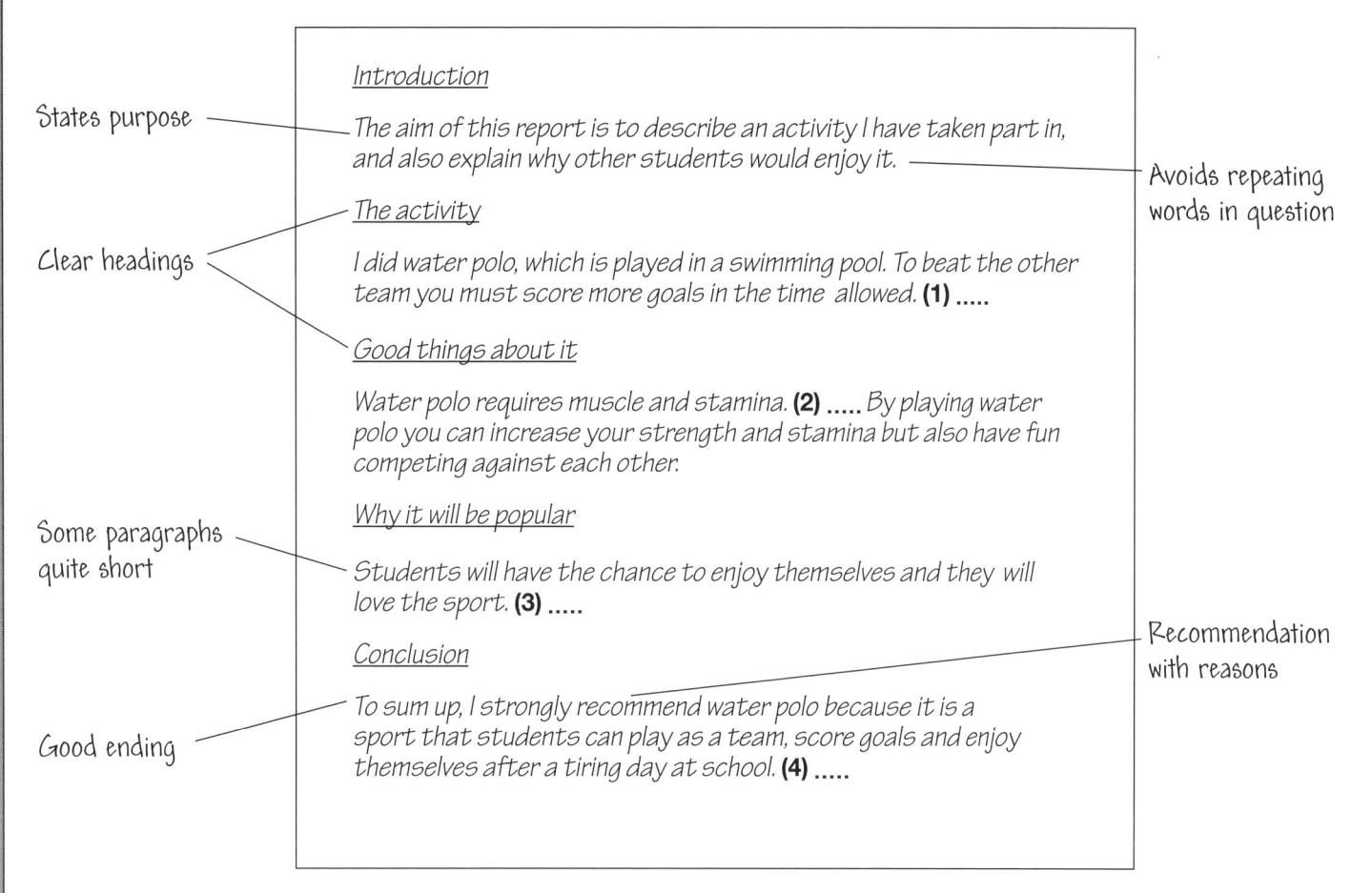

States purpose —

Clear headings —

Some paragraphs quite short —

Good ending —

Introduction

The aim of this report is to describe an activity I have taken part in, and also explain why other students would enjoy it.

The activity

I did water polo, which is played in a swimming pool. To beat the other team you must score more goals in the time allowed. **(1)** .....

Good things about it

Water polo requires muscle and stamina. **(2)** ..... By playing water polo you can increase your strength and stamina but also have fun competing against each other.

Why it will be popular

Students will have the chance to enjoy themselves and they will love the sport. **(3)** .....

Conclusion

To sum up, I strongly recommend water polo because it is a sport that students can play as a team, score goals and enjoy themselves after a tiring day at school. **(4)** .....

— Avoids repeating words in question

— Recommendation with reasons

3 Study the notes next to Tomasz's report. Then add sentences A–D in the correct gaps 1–4.

A I therefore suggest it should become a college sport.
B In addition, it would appear that there are no local water polo clubs.
C Although this is only 30 minutes, for the players it seems much longer.
D In fact, it is said to be the most physically demanding of all sports.

4 Read the completed report.
1 Is it either too short or too long for Writing Part 2?
2 Is it well organised? How many paragraphs does it have?
3 Does it answer both parts of the question? In which paragraphs?
4 Is it written in an appropriate style?
5 Are there any language errors?
6 Which expressions from *Useful language* on page 76 does the writer use?
7 Do you think this report would get full marks?

Writing Part 2 (report)

Test 2 Exam practice — Writing Part 2 (report)

Action plan

1 Read the instructions. Do you know enough facts about the topic to write a report on it?
2 Decide who will read your report and what they will want to know.
3 Think about any knowledge and/or personal experience you could mention, and note down some ideas.
4 Decide if you will use headings, and think of a good title that indicates the content of the report.
5 Spend a few minutes making a plan based on all parts of the task, including recommendations or suggestions.
6 Write your text in a style that is appropriate for your readers. Try to make it interesting; if possible, include some facts that may be new to them.

Tip! In your first paragraph, say what the purpose of the report is.

7 Try to use expressions from *Useful language* on page 76 in each part of your report.

1 Read the exam task below.

1 Who is your report for?
2 What *two* things do you have to do?

Tip! Remember that in Part 2 you can write up to 180 words – 30 more than in Part 1.

> You have had a class discussion about traffic problems in your country, and your teacher has asked you to write a report on transport where you live. Describe the forms of public transport available in your area, and suggest how they could be improved.

2 Write your report.

Tip! Remember to organise your work into paragraphs and insert headings if you think it will be clearer.

Test 2 Training — Writing Part 2 (review)

◀ **Page 24** *Writing Part 2 information*

Task information (review)

- The review task in Part 2 tests your ability to describe something you have experienced (e.g. a TV programme or a product) and give your opinion of it, with a recommendation to the reader.
- You read a description of a situation and then write a review of it in 120–180 words. You should allow about 40 minutes for this task, including time at the end to check your work.
- The instructions also tell you where your review will be published (e.g. in a student newsletter). You therefore have to write in an appropriate style.
- You need to organise your text into paragraphs.
- You should write full sentences and try to use correct grammar, punctuation and spelling and a good range of language.

Useful language: review

1 Match the headings in the box with groups of expressions 1–4.

| Criticising   Advising not to do something   Recommending   Praising |

1 ....
I was pleased to see that …
… was even better than we had expected
It was a nice surprise to find that …
The … was absolutely perfect, and …
We had (a pleasant/an enjoyable/a marvellous, etc.) time at …
It was one of the best … I have ever …

2 ....
We were (rather) disappointed to find that …
There should have been …
The advertisement said that … but in fact …
There wasn't any … at all
I thought there was going to be … but there was only …
There weren't enough … to … / it was too … to …

3 ....
If you get the chance to … (see it/buy one/go there, etc.), … I would advise …
Don't miss the opportunity to …
Anyone who likes … will really enjoy …
I'm sure everyone will find … worth (listening to/visiting/trying, etc.).

4 ....
I (would) suggest finding a better … than this, such as …
My advice is to avoid this … and … instead.
I (would strongly) advise against (watching/reading/eating, etc.) this …

2 Complete the sentences with contrast links. Use each word once.

| however   spite   although   even   despite |

1 ….. the concert started on time, it finished early.
2 It rained every day. ….. this, we all enjoyed our holiday.
3 The theme park has some excellent rides. ….. , the queues were very long.
4 It's a good film, in ….. of the poor acting at times.
5 I would certainly read this book again, ….. though it is 800 pages long.

3 Rewrite 1–5 so that the second sentence means the same as the first.

1 It was late at night, but the club was still empty.
   The club was still empty, even ....
2 The traffic was heavy, but we arrived on time.
   In spite ....
3 We asked twice for coffee, but the waiter didn't bring it.
   Although ....
4 We were a long way from the stage, but I could hear every word they said.
   Even ....
5 The bed was too short, but I would still recommend this hotel.
   Despite ....

Writing Part 2 (review)

Understanding instructions

1 Study the exam instructions below and underline the key words.
   1 What situation do you have to think about?
   2 Who are you going to write a review for? What style of writing is suitable?
   3 What two things do the instructions say you must do?
   4 What else should you add?

> **Reviews wanted!**
>
> What did you think of the last holiday home you stayed in? Write a review of a house or apartment anywhere in the world for our popular website for travellers and tourists. Describe the holiday home and say why you did or did not enjoy your stay there.
>
> Interesting reviews will appear on our site within 24 hours.

2 Quickly read the model review below. Did the writer enjoy staying in the apartment?

3 Study the text and the notes more carefully.
   1 What reasons does the writer give for enjoying being there? What advice does s/he give?
   2 What adjectives (words and phrases) describe the apartment and the building?
   3 Which contrast links are used? Which other linking expressions can you find?
   4 Which expressions similar to those in *Useful language* on page 79 does the writer use (e.g. *spent a pleasant fortnight at ...*)?

Model review

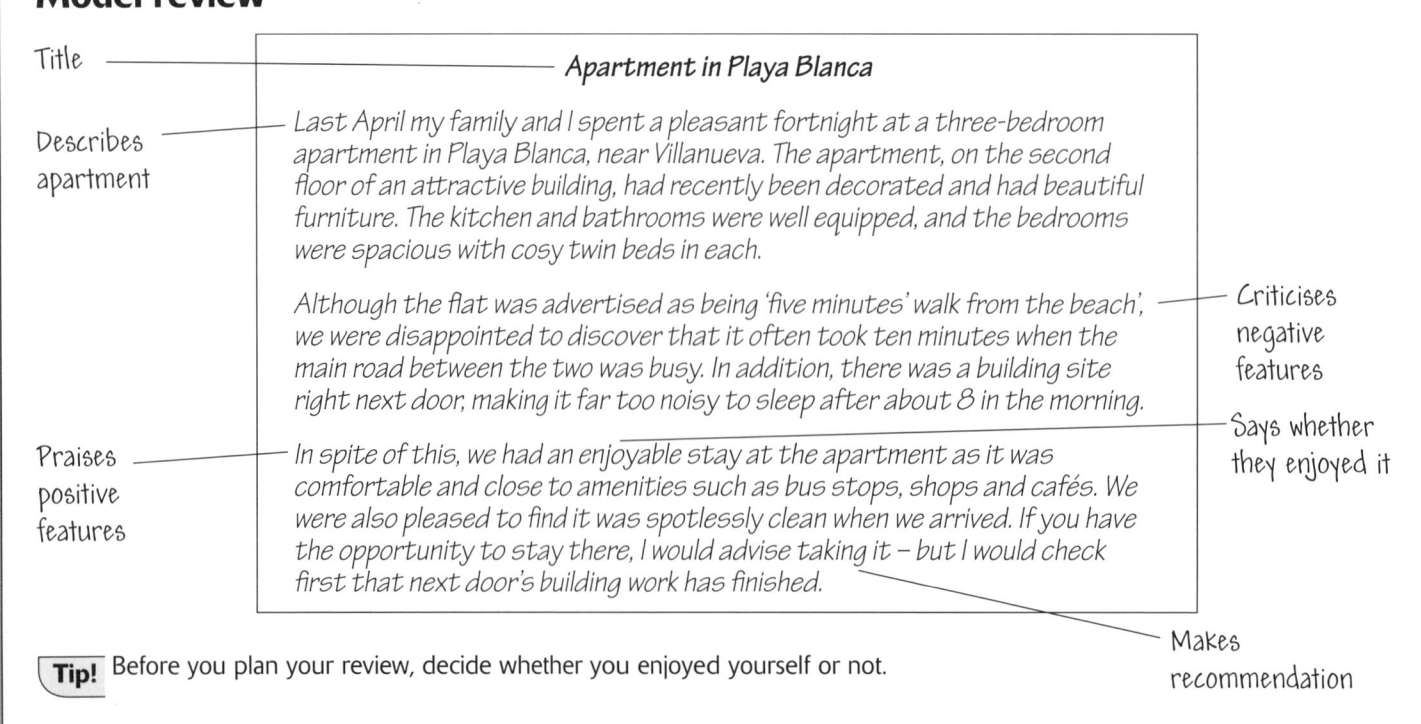

Title — *Apartment in Playa Blanca*

Describes apartment — Last April my family and I spent a pleasant fortnight at a three-bedroom apartment in Playa Blanca, near Villanueva. The apartment, on the second floor of an attractive building, had recently been decorated and had beautiful furniture. The kitchen and bathrooms were well equipped, and the bedrooms were spacious with cosy twin beds in each.

Although the flat was advertised as being 'five minutes' walk from the beach', we were disappointed to discover that it often took ten minutes when the main road between the two was busy. In addition, there was a building site right next door, making it far too noisy to sleep after about 8 in the morning. — *Criticises negative features*

Praises positive features — In spite of this, we had an enjoyable stay at the apartment as it was comfortable and close to amenities such as bus stops, shops and cafés. We were also pleased to find it was spotlessly clean when we arrived. If you have the opportunity to stay there, I would advise taking it – but I would check first that next door's building work has finished. — *Says whether they enjoyed it*

— *Makes recommendation*

Tip! Before you plan your review, decide whether you enjoyed yourself or not.

Test 2 Exam practice / Writing Part 2 (review)

Action plan

1. Read the instructions and try to think of something relevant that you have seen, heard or read to review. Or just use your imagination.
2. Think about who the readers of your review will be and what they will want to know.
3. Note down some points to mention, and spend a few minutes making a plan that includes description, explanation and recommendation. Decide how many paragraphs you will use.
4. Give your review a title that tells readers what it is about.
5. Write your text in a style that is appropriate for the publication and the readers.
6. Use some of the expressions from *Useful language* on page 79 to praise or to criticise.
7. Use some of the contrast links in Exercises 2 and 3 on page 79 to describe unexpected things, or to make both positive and negative points.
8. Finish by recommending or advising readers against the subject of your review (e.g. *it would make the perfect day out for young people*).

1 Read the exam task below.

 1 Who is your review for?
 2 What *three* things do you have to do?

You recently saw this notice in an English-language magazine.

> **Reviews wanted!**
>
> Our magazine is going to include a new section called 'Popular music sites'. If there is an internet music site that you visit often, why not write a review of it? In your review, describe the site, say what you think of it and whether you would recommend it to other people.
>
> The three best reviews will be published in our new music section next week.

2 Write your review.

Tip! Try to include some interesting facts and lively comments in your review.

Test 2 Training — Writing Part 2 (short story)

◄ **Page 24** *Writing Part 2 information*

Task information (short story)

- The short story task in Part 2 tests your ability to write a text of 120–180 words with a good storyline that will interest readers. Allow about 40 minutes for this task, including time at the end to check your work.
- You need to use narrative verb tenses (e.g. past simple, past continuous and past perfect) and linking expressions.
- There is a sentence in the instructions which you have to use in your story.
- You may need to write in the first person (*I*), or about somebody else (*he/she/they*).
- You need to plan the content of each paragraph.
- You should write full sentences. Try to use correct grammar, spelling and punctuation, and a variety of language – particularly adjectives and adverbs.

Useful language: short story

1 Complete the text about writing narratives with these verb forms.

past perfect   past simple   past continuous

When you're writing a story, particularly the first paragraph when you're setting the scene, you can use a variety of tenses to make it more interesting. For events, the most common form is the **(1)** ..... (e.g. *Marta saw a light ahead*) but to describe the background we often use the **(2)** ..... (e.g. *Marta was listening to music on her MP3 player, when suddenly …*). When you're already talking about the past, but you want to mention something that happened before something else, you can use the **(3)** ..... (e.g. *Unfortunately, Marta had left her mobile phone at home*).

2 Complete these sentences with a suitable past form of the verbs in brackets.

1 A tall, well-dressed woman .... (stand) by the hotel entrance, and after thinking for a moment, I .... (remember) where I .... (see) her once before.
2 I .... (watch) TV when I .... (hear) the alarm, but by the time the police .... (arrive) the three men .... (escape) down a side street.
3 This morning as I .... (walk) along the road, I .... (see) the man who .... (try) to steal my bag the night before. I .... (recognise) him even though he .... (wear) a suit, whereas the night before he .... (look) quite different in a T-shirt and jeans.

Understanding instructions

1 Study the exam instructions below and underline the key words.

1 Who has asked you to write the story?
2 Where will it be published?

> Your teacher has asked you to write a story for the school's English-language magazine. Your story must **begin** with the following words:
>
> *Samantha had expected bad news, but when she left the room she was smiling.*
>
> Write your **story**.

82 | Test 2 Training   Writing Part 2 (short story)

2 👁 **Quickly read this First Certificate candidate's story and the notes next to it.**
  1 Does the candidate use the prompt sentence in the right place? Does it fit into the story well?
  2 Which paragraphs create suspense?
  3 What kind of ending does the story have?

Good title

Direct speech for her thoughts

Describes a developing mystery

Final paragraph explains the mystery

The big surprise

Samantha had expected bad news, but when she left the room she was smiling. 'I must tell mum and dad about it!' she thought happily. Samantha went home. Although it was pouring with rain, she didn't notice because she was so busy thinking about her future.

As she opened the door the house was strangely silent. At her home it's never silent at four in the afternoon. 'Where are my brothers? Where are my parents?' she asked herself. Samantha shouted their names, she ran upstairs and downstairs, but her family weren't there. It seemed that they had completely disappeared!

But a moment later she heard a noise. 'What's that?' she wondered. It was getting louder and louder and suddenly she realised where it was coming from. There was someone in the garage. Terrified, Samantha opened the door.

And there she saw her family, saying 'Congratulations!'

Samantha was astonished. 'How did you know I had passed my final examinations?' she asked eventually. 'Your headteacher phoned and told me about your excellent results. So we've organised this party for you. Congratulations, Samantha!' her mum said proudly. In the end it was the happiest day of Samantha's life.

Describes how she felt at the beginning

A short sentence to build up suspense

Direct speech brings characters to life

3 Find at least two examples of each of these techniques in the story.
  1 Use of the past perfect for an earlier event
  2 Use of the past continuous for the background
  3 Expressions that introduce surprising events
  4 Interesting adjectives or adverbs to describe how people felt
  5 Expressions that introduce final events

Test 2 Exam practice — Writing Part 2 (short story)

◀ Page 24 *Writing Part 2 information*

Action plan

1 Read the instructions to find out where to use the given sentence.
2 Decide whether you have to write in the first person (*I*), the third person (*he/she/they*), or whether you can choose. If you can choose, make your choice now.
3 Think about who your readers will be and what kind of story might interest them.
4 Think about how you will end your story. Will the ending be happy, sad – or a mystery?
5 Spend a few minutes planning your story, making sure you have a clear beginning, middle and end.

Tip! To get ideas for your story, ask yourself questions beginning *Who …? What …? Where …? When …? How …?* and *Why …?*

6 Think of a good title for your story.
7 Begin with a description that sets the scene and makes readers want to know more.
8 Don't introduce too many characters. With a 180-word limit, you won't be able to develop them properly.
9 Don't forget to use some of the expressions from *Useful language* on page 82.
10 To keep your readers interested, use 'suspense' – the feeling of excitement when you think something is going to happen.
11 Use a variety of past tenses and try to include some direct speech to bring your story to life (e.g. *'Don't tell anyone else about this,'* he warned).
12 Try to use some interesting adjectives, adverbs and expressions.

---

1 Read the exam task below.

1 Why are you writing the story?
2 Where must you use the words given?

> You have decided to enter a short story competition in an English-language magazine. The competition rules say that your story must **begin** with the following words:
>
> *It was only a small mistake but it changed my life …*

2 Write your story.

Tip! If you invent a character, imagine details such as age, appearance and character before you begin writing about them.

Tip! Describe how the main character felt at different points in the story, and say what they saw, heard or touched.

Test 2 Exam practice — Writing Part 2 (set texts – question 5)

◀ **Page 24** *Writing Part 2 information*
◀ **Page 27** *Action plan (letter)*
◀ **Page 31** *Action plan (essay)*

Task information (set texts)

- Question 5 in Part 2 tests your ability to write a text (e.g. *essay*) of 120–180 words based on your knowledge of one or two books, which usually change every two years.
- Allow about 40 minutes for this task, including time at the end to check your work.
- One of these books is normally a classic; the other is more recent – often a thriller or science-fiction book.

- There is one question about each book. You can choose either, but it is best not to do question 5 unless you have a good knowledge of the book.
- Possible task types are: article, essay, letter, report or review.

Answer **one** of the following two questions based on **one** of the set texts.

(a) *Pride and Prejudice* – Jane Austen

As in any novel, there are good and bad characters in *Pride and Prejudice*. Which one did you like best, and why?

Write your **essay**.

(b) *Great Expectations* – Charles Dickens

Read this part of a letter from your English-speaking friend, Ruby.

Which do you think is the most interesting scene in 'Great Expectations'? Why?

Write a **letter** to her, giving your opinion.

Tip! Remember that in your essay you can choose to write for or against the statement – or present the arguments on both sides.

Tip! Where possible, your main paragraphs should all contain more than one sentence.

Test 2 Training — PAPER 3 Use of English Part 1

◄ Page 35 *Task information*
◄ Page 37 *Action plan*

Useful language: collocations

1 Choose the correct alternative in *italics*.

1 Eating badly can result *on/in* poor health.
2 That old city is known *for/of* its beautiful castle.
3 My teacher is still not satisfied *with/of* my work.
4 Hannah is proud *of/for* her daughter's success.
5 It takes time to get used *to/of* living in another country.
6 The film is based *of/on* events that really happened.
7 I was disappointed *for/with* the food in that café.
8 Leroy is capable *of/in* running 100 metres in under 10 seconds.

2 Add a verb in the correct form to complete the collocations.

1 I .... the last bus home so I had to walk.
2 I'm happy because my team .... yesterday's match 5–0.
3 On Sunday afternoons I often stay at home and .... cards with my family.
4 Please .... this secret. Don't tell anyone.
5 I'll get a car if I .... my driving test.
6 The directors are .... a meeting next week.
7 Last winter I .... a bad cold.
8 Some footballers .... lots of money every week.

3 ◉ Choose A, B, C or D in these sentences written by First Certificate candidates, and say why each is correct.

1 He wanted to … off the appointment until next Wednesday.
   A put   B make   C turn   D leave
2 We heard a … noise and part of the old building collapsed.
   A loud   B strong   C high   D heavy
3 I agree … one point with Chris: it will be hard for us to walk 80 km.
   A in   B of   C on   D for
4 We should give teenagers a place to … up their own club.
   A make   B set   C put   D stand
5 You have to change your general … to life.
   A attitude B opinion C view   D feeling
6 People doing that job should be well paid. But, as … as I know, they're not.
   A much   B long   C far   D good
7 I must … on paying for the phone calls I made from your flat.
   A demand   B suggest C require D insist
8 At that restaurant they treat you … if you were a princess.
   A almost   B as   C just   D so

> **Tip!** For each gap, look at the whole sentence before you choose the answer.

Advice

1 Which option can you add to 'off' to mean 'postpone to a future time'?

2 Which adjective collocates with 'noise'?

3 Which preposition follows 'agree' when it means 'have the same opinion about something'?

4 You need to complete a phrasal verb with 'up' that means 'get everything ready'.

5 Only one of these nouns is followed by 'to'.

6 Which word completes a set phrase meaning 'I think it's true but I'm not sure'?

7 Only one of these verbs is followed by 'on'.

8 Which forms a set phrase with 'if', for something that only seems to be true?

Test 2 Exam practice — Use of English Part 1

Page 37 *Action plan*

Follow the exam instructions, using the advice to help you.

Tip! Understanding the overall meaning of the text makes it easier to choose the right words for the gaps.

For questions **1–12**, read the text below and decide which answer (**A**, **B**, **C** or **D**) best fits each gap. There is an example at the beginning (**0**).

Example:

0   A reporting   B quoting   C according   D informing

| 0 | A | B | C | D |

Advice

0 This completes the preposition 'according to', which here means 'as shown by'.

Fingernails growing faster

People's fingernails and toenails, **(0)** ..... to a recent study, are nowadays growing more quickly. Research **(1)** ..... out at the University of North Carolina indicates that the speed at which human nails are growing has increased by **(2)** ..... to 25 per cent over the last 70 years.

The results of the study show that the **(3)** ..... human fingernail now grows about 3.5 mm a month, **(4)** ..... with just 3 mm seven decades ago. Toenail growth, **(5)** ..... only about 2 mm per month, was also up on the figure **(6)** ..... in a similar survey done 70 years ago.

Researchers **(7)** ..... the rapid increase down to changes in lifestyle, particularly the greater **(8)** ..... of the importance of regular exercise and a healthy diet. This, they point out, is in **(9)** ..... with similar trends in the height and weight of present-day adults.

Interestingly, it appears that nails **(10)** ..... to grow fastest in warmer conditions, with the quickest growth **(11)** ..... among young people, and men. The fastest-growing nail is on the middle finger, while that on the little finger is **(12)** ..... far the slowest, at only a fraction over 3 mm each month.

1 This one completes a phrasal verb which means 'done'.

2 Only one of these completes an expression meaning 'almost'.

3 Which word usually goes with figures like '3.5 mm'?

4 Read on to 'seven decades ago'. Which of these words is often followed by 'with'?

5 Only one of these linking words can go with 'only about 2 mm per month'.

6 Which word forms a collocation with 'figure' and fits the grammar of the sentence?

1	A taken	B carried	C studied	D worked
2	A near	B just	C close	D next
3	A average	B medium	C common	D standard
4	A opposed	B measured	C related	D compared
5	A although	B despite	C however	D nevertheless
6	A achieved	B concluded	C arrived	D obtained
7	A set	B write	C put	D say
8	A belief	B information	C familiarity	D awareness
9	A way	B rule	C line	D case
10	A tend	B lean	C head	D aim
11	A pace	B rate	C speed	D step
12	A by	B so	C as	D too

Tip! Remember to look for prepositions that often follow certain verbs and adjectives.

Test 2 Training — Use of English Part 2

Page 39 *Task information*

Useful language: relative pronouns, auxiliary verbs and reference words

1 Complete the sentences using each word once.

| any | be | despite | did | during | it |
| round | so | what | whereas | | |

1 This mountain is considered to ..... one of the most difficult to climb in the world.
2 Some parents would rather their children ..... not have to take so many exams.
3 As he walked onto the stage his mind went blank and he couldn't think ..... to say.
4 We enjoyed our day at the beach, ... which we swam several times.
5 I have been intending to do this job for ages, but I just haven't got ..... to it yet.
6 The planet Venus is very hot, ... Mars is extremely cold.
7 We needed some more milk, but there wasn't ..... left in the fridge.
8 My mother went to that school and ..... did I. My daughter will, too.
9 Diamonds and other jewellery are still popular, ... the high prices.
10 I don't think ..... makes sense to keep spending so much money.

2 👁 Three of the underlined words in these sentences written by First Certificate candidates are correct. Correct the seven words that are wrong.

1 Certain animals couldn't survive, <u>owing</u> to the lack of food.
2 The first group, <u>which</u> performance started at midday, was the best.
3 <u>They</u> are still so many unexplained events which need to be cleared up.
4 People who live in city centres have to put up <u>with</u> polluted air and noise all the time.
5 It was a beautiful vase, and I have been looking for <u>same</u> like that.
6 I hope we will see <u>each</u> other as soon as possible.
7 Later, I realised it was the worst thing <u>it</u> could have happened to me.
8 Unfortunately, they do not have <u>nothing</u> at all in common with each other.
9 You can come in September, <u>where</u> courses mostly start.
10 I have lived in Spain since 1997, <u>what</u> means I left Colombia when I was one.

Test 2 Exam practice / Use of English Part 2

Page 41 *Action plan*

Follow the exam instructions, using the advice to help you.

Tip! Remember always to read the whole text before you try to fill in *any* gaps.

For questions **13–24**, read the text below and think of the word which best fits each gap. Use only **one** word in each gap. There is an example at the beginning (**0**).

Example: | 0 | I | N |

How the Tour de France began

The very first Tour de France, the greatest cycle race **(0)** ..in.. the world, was held in 1903. It began when two French journalists, Henri Desgrange and Géo Lefèvre, came **(13)** ..... with the idea of a race right round the country, **(14)** ..... that had never been tried anywhere before.

Nowadays we might think the aim of **(15)** ..... an idea would be to bring in lots of television money, or even tourists, but at the beginning of the twentieth century what they wanted to do **(16)** ..... sell more copies of their newspaper. And they succeeded. Circulation figures, **(17)** ..... had been 25,000, went to 65,000 within a year, and on to half a million by 1923.

The reporters were in fact quite closely involved in organising the race, and Desgrange would go **(18)** ..... to remain Tour Director from 1903 right up to 1939. Even **(19)** ..... , their initial design for the race changed in several important ways before the first one was run. For instance, they had intended **(20)** ..... to be held over five weeks, but such a long race was just too much for most riders and very **(21)** ..... wanted to take part.

So it became half **(22)** ..... length, and it would be run entirely in July **(23)** ..... than from late May to early July. As, however, it would still go right round France, the distance travelled each day would be much longer, with cyclists sometimes **(24)** ..... to ride at night.

Tip! Some answers may be auxiliary verbs like *has* or *will*.

Tip! If you can't think of an answer, make the best guess you can. You may be right.

Advice

13 This completes a 3-part phrasal verb meaning 'thought of'.

14 A subject is needed before 'that', but it must be just one word.

15 A word that often goes with 'a' or 'an' is needed, so the phrase means 'an idea like this'.

16 A verb is needed, but in what tense?

17 This completes a non-defining relative clause. Which pronoun is needed?

18 This completes a phrasal verb which means 'continue'.

Test 2 Training — Use of English Part 3

◀ Page 42 *Task information*

Useful language: word formation

1 Complete the sentences with the correct form of the word in capitals. Look carefully at the words before and after each gap and decide what part of speech you need.

1	I was ..... when I heard I had won a holiday in Acapulco!	**DELIGHT**
2	We've got ..... coming to our house later this evening.	**VISIT**
3	The ..... mountain in Africa is Mount Kilimanjaro, which is 5,895 metres.	**HIGH**
4	In the mountains, it's much ..... to travel by horse than by bicycle.	**EASY**
5	Nowadays many people ..... travelling by plane and prefer to take the train.	**LIKE**
6	The old house is nearly falling down and it's completely	**INHABIT**
7	There are restrictions on car use in a ..... number of cities.	**GROW**
8	The most ..... countryside here is in the river valley. It's beautiful.	**ATTRACT**
9	Clothes are important in this nightclub and people are always ..... dressed.	**FASHION**
10	The owner of that island is extremely ..... ; he's worth a billion dollars.	**WEALTH**

2 👁 **Correct the mistakes made by First Certificate candidates.**
1. Now I'm working as a shop assistent.
2. I went there quite happyly for the first school day.
3. Thank you for your kind hospitality and warmness.
4. Going to work or to school by bike is very healthful.
5. It was my first job and I felt very exciting!
6. Our tourist office is not able to promote the city's attractives.
7. I prefer to read books that are inusual in some way.
8. The fitness plan explains how you can put on weigt.
9. The doctor told the patient he could get more air by breathing more slowlier.
10. The car has its advantages, such as proteccion from bad weather.

Tip! Remember always to check your spelling!

Advice

1 'I was' is followed here by an adjective. What form do we use to describe how someone feels?

2 A noun is required, but is it singular or plural? There are two noun forms for this word – which do we need here? ('... coming to our house' should tell you!)

3 An adjective is needed. What form might follow 'the'? The use of a number is a clue.

4 What does 'than' tell you about the missing word? Be careful with the spelling.

5 If they 'prefer' to do something else, is the missing verb likely to be positive or negative? Is a prefix or a suffix required?

6 The missing word describes 'house'. What does 'nearly falling down' tell you about the meaning? You need to add both a prefix and suffix here.

Test 2 Exam practice — Use of English Part 3

◀ **Page 44** *Action plan*

1 Quickly read the title and the text in the exam task below. What is it about?

2 Look at the example (0) and read these points.
   - The missing word comes before the noun *city*, so it is probably an adjective of nationality.
   - AMERICA can form the adjective *American*, with a capital *A*, by adding *n*.

3 Follow the exam instructions. For each of 25–34, study the gap, the sentence it is in and the word in capitals.

For questions **25–34**, read the text below. Use the word given in capitals at the end of some of the lines to form a word that fits in the gap **in the same line**. There is an example at the beginning (**0**).

Example: | 0 | A | M | E | R | I | C | A | N | | | | | | | |

The city of Miami

The (0) *American* city of Miami was founded in 1896 by Julia Tuttle, a (25) ..... Florida businesswoman. From a population then of just 300, it has become a vast urban area of 5.5 million (26) ....., attracting (27) ..... from all over the world. Its excellent transport links mean it can (28) ..... be reached by road, rail, air or sea.

The city's continuing (29) ..... as a tourist and financial centre has led to a construction boom. Many of the new buildings are over 120 metres in (30) ....., giving Miami the most impressive skyline in the country after New York and Chicago.

Its wide variety of (31) ..... includes sandy beaches, nightclubs, music and dancing, as well as activities such as skateboarding and cycling in the world-famous, (32) ..... South Beach area. The city centre has a number of (33) ..... parks and gardens, and of course there is the wonderful weather: (34) ..... any other major city in the USA, it has a genuinely tropical climate.

AMERICA
WEALTH
INHABIT
VISIT
EASY

GROW

HIGH

ATTRACT

FASHION
DELIGHT
LIKE

Advice

25 *'Florida businesswoman'* is a noun phrase, so an adjective is needed.

26 You need to add a suffix to form a noun from this verb.

27 Attracting who or what? How is the noun formed, and will it be singular or plural?

28 What kind of word often comes before a verb? Be careful with the spelling.

Tip! Remember to use the context, especially the words next to the gap, to work out what kind of word you need to form (e.g. *noun, plural*).

Tip! Remember you always have to change the word given, and that you can use a prefix *and* a suffix.

Test 2 Training — Use of English Part 4

<Page 45 *Task information*

Useful language: reported speech, linking words, conditionals, etc.

1 Complete the second sentence so that it means the same as the first. In each case, underline the words that change in both sentences.

Note: this is not an exam task and there is no key word.

1 On Saturday night, I hate staying in by myself.
  On Saturday night, I hate staying in on ....
2 Despite the fact I was carrying an umbrella, I got completely wet.
  I got completely wet, even ....
3 Harry is sorry he didn't get up earlier yesterday morning.
  Harry wishes he ....
4 People believe it was the worst storm in history.
  It is believed to ....
5 Somebody has painted our house.
  We have had ....
6 It's years since I swam in the sea.
  I haven't ....
7 'Are you going to the party?' Ingrid asked me.
  Ingrid asked me ....
8 I couldn't find Callum's address so I didn't write to him.
  If I hadn't lost Callum's address, I ....

2 Choose the correct words in *italics* in these sentences written by First Certificate candidates.

1 After ten minutes the waiter asked me if I *want/wanted* to eat.
2 If you haven't done any exercise *for/since* a long time, try to increase it gradually.
3 We had a wonderful evening. I wish you *were/had been* there with us.
4 *Even if/Even though* I am very fond of my bicycle, it is impossible to ride it in a big modern city.
5 Our local council is said *has/to have* spent no money at all on improvements.
6 You can go to a sports club, but there are also many things you can do *on/by* your own.
7 I've just had *my hair cut/cut my hair* and changed my wardrobe.
8 If you had really been there, you would *have not/not have* written the article like that.

Test 2 Exam practice — Use of English Part 4

Page 47 *Action plan*

1 Study the first sentence in questions 35–42 below. For each sentence, underline the words you think you will have to change. (0) has been done as an example.

Tip! Don't write the whole sentence on your answer sheet, just the missing words and key word. When you've finished, read the first sentence again, then the one you have written. Have you got **all** the ideas from the first sentence in your new sentence?

2 Follow the exam instructions.

For questions **35–42**, complete the second sentence so that it has a similar meaning to the first sentence, using the word given. **Do not change the word given**. You must use between **two** and **five** words, including the word given. Here is an example (**0**).

0   We have <u>arranged everything</u> for your trip to China.

  MADE

  We have ………………………………………… your trip to China.

The gap can be filled by the words 'made all the arrangements for', so you write:

Example: | 0 | MADE ALL THE ARRANGEMENTS FOR |

Advice

35 I regret not buying that bike when I had the chance.
  WISH
  I ………………………………………… that bike when I had the chance.

36 In spite of the heavy snow, we managed to get home quickly.
  EVEN
  We managed to get home quickly, ………………………………………… heavily.

37 'Did you see that film on Friday night?' Sean asked me.
  SEEN
  Sean wanted to know ………………………………………… that film on Friday night.

38 I'm afraid you're not old enough to travel abroad by yourself.
  OWN
  You're not old enough to travel abroad ………………………………………… , I'm afraid.

39 Jenny rang because she was worried about us.
  RUNG
  Jenny ………………………………………… she hadn't been worried about us.

40 Have they repaired your computer yet?
  HAD
  Have ………………………………………… yet?

41 It's been a long time since I last ate fish.
  EATEN
  I ………………………………………… a long time.

42 Everyone thinks that the band has split up.
  THOUGHT
  The band ………………………………………… up.

35 We use 'regret' + '-ing' for something in the past. What verb tense follows 'wish' when we talk about an event in the past?

36 The adverb 'heavily' tells you that a verb is needed, but in what tense and form?

37 Study the tense of the verb 'did you see … ?'. What happens to that tense in reported speech?

38 What 3-word expression with 'own' means the same as 'by yourself'?

Test 2 Exam practice / PAPER 4 Listening Part 1

◄ **Page 49** *Task information*
◄ **Page 50** *Action plan*

1 Read the first line of questions 1–8 on page 95. For each one, answer these questions.
   1 What is the situation?
   2 Will you hear one female, one male, or two speakers?

2 What is the focus of the question in the second line?

   Example: *question 1: attitude*

   Tip! Read the question and try to imagine the situation. Who's talking to whom? Where? Why? When? How do they feel?

3 🎧 14 Follow the exam instructions on page 95, using the advice to help you.

   Tip! Remember that you can change your mind about an answer while you listen for the first or the second time.

You will hear people talking in eight different situations. For questions **1–8**, choose the best answer (**A**, **B** or **C**).

1 You hear a woman and a man talking about taking up sailing.
   What does the woman say about it?

   A   it's too expensive
   B   it's too difficult
   C   it's too dangerous

2 You overhear a man talking on the phone in a hospital.
   Who is he?

   A   a doctor
   B   a visitor
   C   a patient

3 You hear a young person talking about an interest she has.
   Where is she?

   A   a bookshop
   B   a museum
   C   a library

4 You hear a teacher talking to a student.
   Why is she talking to him?

   A   to warn him not to do something
   B   to offer to help him do something
   C   to suggest he should do something

5 You overhear a man and a woman talking about meeting two other people.
   Where are these people going to meet their friends?

   A   at a restaurant
   B   at a hotel
   C   in the street

6 You overhear a woman speaking on the phone about her apartment.
   Why is she talking to the other person?

   A   to deny an accusation
   B   to make a complaint
   C   to refuse to do something

7 You hear two young people talking about going to the coast for the day.
   What do they agree about?

   A   the disadvantages of the bus
   B   the need to set off early
   C   the best route to take

8 You hear a woman being interviewed on the radio.
   Why did she decide to become a lawyer?

   A   to help people in need
   B   to do the same job as her sister
   C   to earn a large salary

Advice

1 Think of words associated with the three adjectives in the options. Do you hear the woman use any of them?

2 Don't choose an answer just because you hear the speaker use the same word, or a form of it.

3 Think about the differences between the three places and listen for something that is normally only possible in one of them.

4 Listen for words often used by speakers to express one of functions A–C.

5 Listen for words associated with each of the three places in A–C.

6 Listen for the speaker's purpose when she uses certain expressions, not just the meanings of particular words and phrases.

7 Listen for expressions that indicate agreement or disagreement.

8 Listen for expressions that introduce reasons for her choosing law as a career.

Listening Part 1

Test 2 Exam practice / Listening Part 2

◀ Page 52 *Task information*

◀ Page 53 *Action plan*

1 Read the exam instructions on page 97.
   1 What kind of recording (e.g. *a talk*) is it?
   2 What's the topic?
   3 Who will you hear?
   4 For each gap, what kind of information (e.g. *a verb, a day of the week*) do you need to listen for?

2 🎧15 Follow the exam instructions, using the advice to help you.

Tip! Only write one answer, even if you can think of two or more good ones.

Tip! There is always plenty of time between each answer for you to write down the missing words.

You will hear part of an interview with a woman called Sophie Doyle, who organises adventure holidays in Australia for teenagers. For questions **9–18**, complete the sentences.

Australian Adventure Holidays

The Australian Adventure Holiday is usually in the month of _____ **9**

In each group there are _____ **10** teenagers plus four leaders.

The price covers everything except _____ **11**

When they visit the islands, they will sleep in a _____ **12**

They will first meet the other young people at the _____ **13**

They will visit the largest _____ **14** island in the world.

They will sleep next to a _____ **15** when they are in the outback.

At the Great Barrier Reef, _____ **16** will be available for those who need them.

From the boat on the river, you will see _____ **17** on the banks.

Teenagers normally stay in touch with people at home by _____ **18**

Advice

9 Make sure you focus on the correct country.

10 Think of words with a similar meaning to 'teenagers'. Don't be misled by numbers you hear for different things.

11 Listen for an expression that means 'except'.

12 Choose the kind of accommodation mentioned for the islands, not elsewhere.

13 Listen for an expression which means 'meet the other young people'.

14 Be careful – she mentions another type of island.

15 Listen for an expression that means 'sleep'.

16 Don't be confused by something that everybody needs.

17 What do you think the 'banks' of a river are? Listen for what can be seen on them, not elsewhere.

18 Don't stop listening after you hear one possible answer – it may be wrong.

Tip! Check your answers are grammatically correct (e.g. singular/plural, verb tense).

Tip! Write clearly, so that you can read your answers later and copy them correctly onto the answer sheet.

Test 2 Exam practice — Listening Part 3

◀ **Page 54** *Task information*
◀ **Page 55** *Action plan*

1 Look at the exam instructions and sentences A–F.

1 What is the topic of the five recordings?
2 What information do you need to listen for?

Tip! Remember that one of sentences A–F isn't needed.

2 🎧 16 Follow the exam instructions, using the advice to help you.

Tip! Don't worry about understanding every word in each recording. It isn't necessary.

You will hear five different people talking about why they decided to live in another country.
For questions **19–23**, choose which of the reasons (**A–F**) each speaker is giving.
Use the letters only once. There is one extra letter which you do not need to use.

A She had lost her job.

B She wanted to earn more money.

C A relative had already moved to the same country.

D She was bored in her home town.

E Her new country had a more pleasant climate.

F She wanted to learn another language.

Speaker 1 — 19
Speaker 2 — 20
Speaker 3 — 21
Speaker 4 — 22
Speaker 5 — 23

Advice

A In what situation do people often lose their jobs? What might the boss say? Make sure the speaker is talking about her own job.

B Listen for 'money' expressions, but don't be misled by references to people other than the speaker herself.

C Make sure the speaker is talking about a relative, not a friend, and that you know who arrived there first.

D Listen for a contrast in the way she felt at different times in her life. Make sure the person is talking about the place she came from, not where she is now.

E Three speakers mention the climate, but only one gives it as a reason for going abroad.

F More than one speaker mentions learning the language, but which gives it as a reason for going there?

Tip! When you check your answers the second time you listen, remember that one mistake may have led to others.

Test 2 Exam practice / Listening Part 4

◀ **Page 56** Task information
◀ **Page 57** Action plan

1 Look at the exam instructions.
1 What kind of recording (e.g. *speech*) is it?
2 What's the topic?
3 Who will you hear?

Tip! Don't choose an answer just because you hear the same word or phrase. Listen for the same *idea*.

2 🎧 02 **Follow the exam instructions, using the advice to help you.**

Tip! For each question, wait until the speaker finishes talking about it before you decide on your answer.

You will hear a radio interview with Greg Manolis, an Australian who collects menus. For questions **24–30**, choose the best answer (**A**, **B** or **C**).

---

24 What kind of menus does Greg collect?
   A   mainly valuable ones
   B   only those of historical interest
   C   any that he finds attractive

25 Greg first became interested in menus when
   A   he went on a sea voyage with his family.
   B   he needed material for his homework.
   C   relatives of his came to live in the country.

26 How, according to Greg, do restaurant owners feel about people taking menus?
   A   They sometimes get a little angry.
   B   They see it as free advertising.
   C   They want to charge for them.

27 Restaurants sometimes contact Greg in order to
   A   offer him a copy of their latest menu.
   B   ask about menus at other restaurants.
   C   invite his family to eat a special meal.

28 Greg talks particularly about a meal he had in an overseas restaurant which served
   A   Indian food.
   B   Scottish food.
   C   Mexican food.

29 His favourite way of buying menus is
   A   on internet auction sites.
   B   through collectors' magazines.
   C   in small specialist shops.

30 Which of Greg's menus is worth the most money?
   A   one from a restaurant owned by a famous singer
   B   one specially made to celebrate a sporting event
   C   one signed by famous Hollywood actors in 1928

Advice

24 Be careful with answers that describe what other people do or say.

25 Make sure you know who did what and when.

26 Be careful that the option you choose actually refers to 'restaurant owners'.

27 Do they want to give Greg something, or do they want him to do something for them?

28 Listen to all he says about this. Don't decide as soon as you hear a word in the options.

29 Listen for words which describe how he feels about one of A–C.

30 Think of ways of saying the opposite of 'is worth the most money'.

Tip! If you're not sure of an answer, mark the two possible options. Choose from those on the second listening.

Listening Part 4

Test 2 Exam practice | 99

Test 2 Training — PAPER 5 Speaking Part 1

◄ **Page 58** *Task information*

Revising expressions

1 For questions 1–6, decide which is the best thing to do in Speaking Part 1: A, B or C.

1 When you go into the room for the Speaking test, you should

   A always use formal language and call the examiners 'Sir' or 'Madam'.
   B be polite and friendly to the examiners and your partner.
   C ignore everyone until the exam questions begin.

2 When the examiner asks you a question, you should

   A just say 'yes', 'no' or 'maybe'.
   B answer with a speech you prepared earlier.
   C give full answers, with reasons and examples.

3 In Part 1, you should always reply to

   A the examiner who asks you the questions.
   B the other candidate.
   C the examiner who does not ask the questions.

4 While the other candidate is speaking, you should

   A listen to what he or she says.
   B think about something else.
   C correct any mistakes he or she makes.

5 If you don't understand a question, you should

   A say nothing.
   B pretend you understand and talk about something else.
   C politely ask the examiner to repeat it.

6 During the test, you

   A can use words in your first language if you need to.
   B must talk only in English.
   C may ask the examiner to translate certain words.

2 If possible, work in pairs. Think of three expressions for:

1 asking for repetition   *Sorry, I didn't catch that.*
2 adding information
3 giving a reason
4 giving an example.

Test 2 Exam practice — Speaking Part 1

Page 59 *Action plan*

If you have a partner, answer these questions in pairs.

Tip! Don't spend *too* long thinking before you reply to the examiner's questions.

Part 1 — 3 minutes (5 minutes for groups of three)

Interlocutor First of all, we'd like to know something about you.

- Where are you from?

- What do you like about living there?

- What is your favourite part of the day? Why?

- What kind of TV programmes do you enjoy? Why?

- What's the best present you've ever received? Why was it so special?

Tip! Think of a different way of saying something if you don't know a particular word.

Tip! Don't worry about getting every factual detail correct (e.g. the exact year you started school). It's a language test, not a job interview!

Test 2 Training — Speaking Part 2

Page 60 *Task information*

Revising expressions

1 Are statements 1–10 about Speaking Part 2 true (T) or false (F)?
Correct the false statements.

1. Each candidate has to discuss two photos.
2. Each candidate has to speak for two minutes.
3. When you see the photos, you should plan what you're going to say.
4. You need to compare the photos and also answer the question about them.
5. You must describe everything you can see in both pictures.
6. You can correct yourself if you make a mistake when you're speaking.
7. You should check your watch to see when you have to stop.
8. You should listen to your partner without interrupting them.
9. You need to be ready to answer a question about your partner's photos.
10. At the end of your partner's turn, you can comment on what s/he has said.

2 If possible, work in pairs. Think of three expressions to:

1. say which picture you're talking about
   The picture on the left shows …
2. compare the pictures
3. contrast the pictures
4. say what you think is possible in the pictures
5. say which of two things you'd prefer to do.

Test 2 Exam practice — Speaking Part 2

Page 62 *Action plan*

1 Look at the exam instructions below and photos A, B, C and D on pages C8–C9.

1 What does each of A–D show?
2 What does Candidate A have to do?
3 What does Candidate B have to do?

Tip! Remember that the examiner will give you spoken instructions for the task, and you can also read them at the top of the page.

Tip! As soon as you see the pictures, start thinking about what you will say, making a mental note of any useful vocabulary you can use. If you're not sure what's in the pictures, don't worry. You can use expressions like *it seems that …, it might be …* or *perhaps …*.

2 If you have a partner, do this exam task in pairs.

Tip! Don't be so worried about making mistakes that you say very little. The examiners can't give you good marks if you don't speak enough.

Part 2

Interlocutor *(Candidate A)*, it's your turn first. Here are your photographs on page C8. They **show people doing different jobs**.

I'd like you to compare the photographs, and say **what they probably like about their jobs**.

(Candidate B), **would you prefer to do a technical job, or work with people?**

Now, *(Candidate B)*, here are your photographs on page C9. **They show people communicating with their friends**.

I'd like you to compare the photographs, and say **what the advantages are of each**.

(Candidate A), **do you use text or email to keep in touch with your friends?**

Tip! When you practise for Part 2, if possible get a friend to time you as you speak. Try to keep going for the full minute!

Test 2 Training — Speaking Part 3

Page 63 *Task information*

Revising expressions

1   Fill in the gaps in this text about Speaking Part 3, using the words in the box. There is one word that you do not need.

agreement	all	decision	each
four	polite	reasons	suggestions
three	top	turns	

In Part 3 you have to speak to your partner for about (1) ..... minutes. The examiner gives you some pictures and explains what you have to do. The instructions are also written at the (2) ..... of the page. Then you discuss (3) ..... picture, taking (4) ..... with your partner so that you both speak for about the same amount of time. At this stage you make (5) ..... , for instance by saying *how about …?*, and give your own opinions, where possible giving (6) ..... to support them. You can disagree with your partner, but if you do, it's important to be (7) ..... . When you have talked about (8) ..... the pictures, you should try to make a (9) ..... about which of them to choose, but in the end it doesn't matter if you can't reach (10) ..... with each other. The important thing is to keep talking for the full length of time.

2   If possible, work in pairs. Think of three expressions to:
   1 make a suggestion
   2 ask if someone agrees with your suggestion
   3 agree with somebody's suggestion
   4 disagree politely with somebody's suggestion
   5 give reasons for disagreeing with somebody's suggestion.

Test 2 Exam practice — Speaking Part 3

Page 64 *Action plan*

1 Study the exam instructions below and the pictures on pages C10–C11.

1 What kind of things do the pictures show?
2 What two things do you have to do?

2 If you have a partner, do this exam task in pairs.

Tip! Take turns with your partner to start talking about each picture. Don't worry if the other candidate seems to know more English than you. Make sure you speak for about the same length of time as him/her.

Tip! You can check with the examiner – or your partner – if you're not sure what you have to do. The instructions are also written above the pictures. Don't try to talk about something different from the topic in the instructions.

Tip! There's no right or wrong decision, and it doesn't matter if you can't agree on one anyway.

Part 3

Interlocutor Now, I'd like you to talk about something together for about three minutes. *(4 minutes for groups of three)*

Here are some pictures of different kinds of natural places.

Show candidates pictures on pages C10–C11.

First, talk to each other about **the attractions of these kinds of places**. Then decide **which two would be the most interesting for a group of young people to visit**.

Test 2 Training — Speaking Part 4

Page 65 *Task information*

Revising expressions; predicting discussion points

1. Choose the correct alternative in *italics* in these sentences about Speaking Part 4.
   1. The topic of Part 4 *links and extends / is different from* the topic of Part 3.
   2. If the examiner asks you a question that you don't understand, you can *see it written down / ask him or her to repeat it.*
   3. If you don't know any facts about the topic, *say what you think about it / say nothing at all.*
   4. During Part 4 you speak to *the other candidate all the time / the person who speaks to you.*
   5. You *are allowed to / are not allowed to* disagree with what your partner says.
   6. You should encourage your partner to say *more / less* about the topic.
   7. You should *take no notice of / listen carefully to* your partner while he or she is speaking.
   8. At the end of the test, you should *shake hands with the examiners / say 'goodbye' and 'thank you' to the examiners.*

2. If possible, work in pairs. Think of three expressions to:
   1. ask for someone's opinion
   2. give your opinion
   3. try to change someone's opinion.

3. Think about the topic of Part 3 (the different kinds of places). What issues do you think the examiner might ask you to discuss?

Tip! Involve your partner in the discussion and give him/her plenty of time to speak.

Test 2 Exam practice — Speaking Part 4

Page 66 *Action plan*

Work in a group of three if possible. Decide who will be the 'examiner' and who will be the 'candidates'. Answer these questions as fully as you can.

Part 4

Interlocutor
- Which areas of countryside would you recommend to visitors to your country? Why?

- How important do you think it is to protect the countryside?

- If you could travel in a very hot or a very cold part of the world, what would you take with you? Why?

Tip! Remember that there are no right or wrong answers or opinions. The important thing is to say what you think!

PAPER 1 Reading Part 1

You are going to read a magazine article about travel guidebooks. For questions **1–8**, choose the answer (**A**, **B**, **C** or **D**) which you think fits best according to the text.

Mark your answers **on the separate answer sheet**.

Writing guidebooks

Nick Inman on where travel guide authors are going.

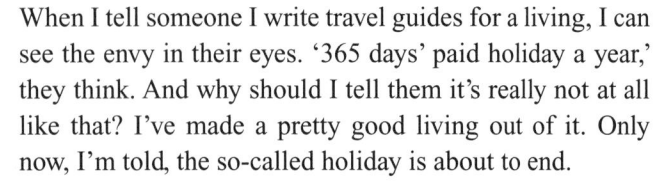

When I tell someone I write travel guides for a living, I can see the envy in their eyes. '365 days' paid holiday a year,' they think. And why should I tell them it's really not at all like that? I've made a pretty good living out of it. Only now, I'm told, the so-called holiday is about to end.

It was widely reported last year that sales of guidebooks are falling fast, thanks to developments in the Internet and mobile phones. It makes sense. Why bother taking a heavy book with you when you can download all the information you need to your phone as you walk around the cathedral?

Writing a new book about a place is a rewarding job, but one that's becoming a rarity. Publishers are more concerned with keeping existing books up to date than bringing out new ones in an already crowded market. This is understandable, since every guidebook is actually out of date as soon as it is published. It may have been researched a year before being printed and it could have sat on the bookshop shelf for a year or two, so its information might be three years old by the time the reader uses it in practice. It is hardly surprising, therefore, that some publishers are investing almost as much in updating and redesigning their books as they did creating them. Updating guides is nowadays a good way for new writers to get started.

But if the Internet via a mobile phone can deliver information just as well as printed paper but much faster, at almost no cost, is there a future for the printed guidebook? Other books you read at home, but a travel guide's main purpose is for urgent reference when you're desperate to find accommodation or somewhere to eat. Using a modern cellphone, any traveller can now enjoy a 'paperless holiday'. Want to know the opening times of the museum? Look them up online. Need some information on the ancient building you're standing in? Download it.

'We did an experiment last year when we went to [FYR*] Macedonia and Serbia,' says Jan Dodd, author of the *Rough Guides* to Vietnam and Japan. 'We had no guidebook but got by fine with internet cafés, using online sources for train information, hotels, even restaurants occasionally. We missed the historical background, but you could probably find that online, too.'

Although sales of some guidebook series are not doing so well, the effects of the IT revolution may not prove as serious as they first seem. People get excited about new technology and forget to think clearly. 'I saw one tourist couple who were carrying around all their downloads in a pile of neat plastic envelopes,' observed Nick Rider, author of Cadogan's Yucatán and Mayan Mexico guides, after a recent trip. 'The fact that people print things out means that the printed word is still very useful, though a good book would actually be much easier to carry around.' And books still have some advantages over computers and mobile phones. Not everyone likes looking at a screen, particularly in bright sunlight. Not everywhere on earth has a reliable internet connection. And who wants to spend all that time in a hotel room recharging batteries?

The Internet's strength of total democracy, enabling anyone to write whatever they like, is also its weakness. 'A huge amount of what's around on the net is boring, unedited, untested, uninformed and untrustworthy,' says Rider. 'Another large percentage of net material is basically advertising, and so equally untrustworthy. Also, internet searches about destinations often produce facts and figures that are years out of date.'

The travel guide will have to adapt to changing travel habits but it isn't finished yet. 'The guidebook is not going to disappear – at least not for a considerable amount of time. That's the general opinion among our members,' says Mary Anne Evans of the Guild of Travel Writers. 'Publishers themselves really do not know what the Internet is capable of, and currently the thinking is that the two will coexist.' Let's hope I'll be 'on holiday' for a good while yet.

*The speaker is referring to the Former Yugoslav Republic of Macedonia.

1   How does Nick Inman feel about his job?

    A   He isn't paid enough money for it.
    B   It is a pity that it has now finished.
    C   He likes being on holiday all the time.
    D   People have the wrong idea about it.

2   What is meant by 'It makes sense' in line 8?

    A   This is partly true.
    B   It is not easy to understand.
    C   This is not surprising.
    D   It is foolish to think that.

3   What does 'did' in line 22 refer to?

    A   updating
    B   investing
    C   creating
    D   redesigning

4   What does Nick Inman suggest about guidebooks in the fourth paragraph?

    A   They contain information that cannot be found elsewhere.
    B   People tend to study them before they set off on a journey.
    C   They are still cheaper than using more modern technology.
    D   People use them when they need information in a hurry.

5   The main purpose of Jan Dodd's experiment was to find out

    A   whether a guidebook was necessary.
    B   facts about the two countries' history.
    C   how good her own guidebook was.
    D   how to travel and where to stay.

6   In Nick Rider's opinion, the two people he observed

    A   had made the best possible use of modern technology.
    B   probably should have taken a guidebook with them.
    C   need not have taken any written tourist information.
    D   had almost certainly printed out the wrong information.

7   Which of the following best describes what Nick Rider says about the Internet?

    A   Its travel advertisements usually give the best information.
    B   It is quite difficult to find reliable travel information there.
    C   Information about the places tourists visit is regularly updated.
    D   The processing of information is not democratic enough.

8   What does Mary Anne Evans say about the future of traveller information?

    A   People will want to use both the Internet and guidebooks.
    B   Publishers are sure the Internet cannot compete with guidebooks.
    C   Before long, guidebooks will no longer be available.
    D   There will always be a demand for guidebooks as they are now.

Reading Part 1

Test 3 — Reading Part 2

You are going to read an article in which the writer looks at the harm done by plastic bags and ways of reducing this. Seven sentences have been removed from the article. Choose from the sentences **A–H** the one which fits each gap (9–15). There is one extra sentence which you do not need to use.

Getting rid of plastic bags by Michael McCarthy

Plastic bags are one of the greatest problems of the consumer society – or to be more precise, of the throwaway society. First introduced in the United States in 1957, and into the rest of the world by the late 1960s, they have been found so convenient that they have come to be used in massive numbers. In the world as a whole, the annual total manufactured now probably exceeds a trillion – that is, one million billion, or 1,000,000,000,000,000.

According to a recent study, whereas plastic bags were rarely seen at sea in the late eighties and early nineties, they are now being found almost everywhere across the planet, from Spitsbergen in the Arctic to the South Atlantic close to Antarctica. They are among the 12 items of rubbish most often found in coastal clean-ups. **9** ☐ Windblown plastic bags are so common in Africa that a small industry has appeared: harvesting bags and using them to make hats and other items, with one group of people collecting 30,000 per month. In some developing countries they are a major nuisance in blocking the drainage systems of towns and villages.

What matters is what happens to them after use. Enormous numbers end up being buried or burnt, which is an enormous waste of the oil products which have gone into their manufacture. **10** ☐ Turtles mistake them for their jellyfish food and choke on them; birds mistake them for fish with similar consequences; dolphins have been found with plastic bags preventing them breathing properly.

The wildlife film-maker Rebecca Hosking was shocked by the effects of the bags on birds on the Pacific island of Midway. She found that two-fifths of the 500,000 albatross chicks born each year die, the vast majority from swallowing plastic that their parents have mistakenly brought back as food. **11** ☐ Many local residents and shopkeepers joined in, and the idea of getting rid of them completely soon spread to other towns and villages.

Although some people remain unconvinced, it does seem possible that the entire country could eventually become plastic-bag free. Who could have imagined half-a-century ago that our public places would one day all become cigarette-smoke free? Or that we would all be using lead-free petrol? Who would have thought even a decade ago, come to that, that about two-thirds of us would by now be actively involved in recycling? **12** ☐

What is needed is a general change in consumer attitudes, towards the habit of using re-usable shopping bags. Older people will remember how this used to be entirely normal as every household had a 'shopping bag', a strong bag which was used to carry items bought in the daily trip to the shops. **13** ☐ Today, many of us tend to drive to the supermarket once a week and fill up the car with seven days' worth of supplies, for which plastic bags, of course, are fantastically useful. It's a hard habit to break.

However, there has already been a big drop in plastic bag use, partly because the leading supermarkets and other shopkeepers are making a major effort to help us give up the habit, with a whole variety of new ideas. **14** ☐ It is clear that habits are starting to change; reusable bags are more visible than they were even two years ago.

Many believe there should be a tax on plastic bags, and the governments of a number of countries are considering the idea. What people have in mind is the example of Ireland, where a tax of €0.22 was introduced on all plastic bags, the first of its kind in the world. **15** ☐ In addition, all the money from the new tax is used for environmental clean-up projects.

A Major changes in public opinion and behaviour can certainly occur.

B On land they are everywhere, too.

C These range from cheap 'bags for life' offers to bag-free check-outs.

D Worse still, billions get into the environment, especially the ocean environment, where they become a terrible threat to wildlife.

E But there was a very different pattern of household shopping then: the purchase of a much smaller number of items, on a daily basis, after a walk to small, local shops.

F She realised then that it was too late to do anything about this man-made disaster.

G This quickly brought about a quite amazing reduction of 90 per cent, from 1.2 billion bags a year to fewer than 200,000 and an enormous increase in the use of cloth bags.

H As a result, she started a movement to turn her home town into the first community in the country to be free of plastic bags.

Test 3 Reading Part 3

You are going to read an article in which four people talk of their experiences of learning languages. For questions **16–30**, choose from the people (**A–D**). The people may be chosen more than once.

Mark your answers **on the separate answer sheet**.

Which person

had tried the same method of study when she was younger?	16
thought her chosen form of study was reasonably priced?	17
found she enjoyed working with other students?	18
believes that she learned from her language mistakes?	19
was aware of the need to stay safe?	20
was unable to write quickly enough?	21
missed going out with people of her own age?	22
eventually found the learning materials she needed?	23
was once embarrassed when she was practising the language?	24
needed to learn the language as quickly as possible?	25
wanted more help with her pronunciation?	26
made a change because she was disappointed with her progress?	27
felt rather tired when she was studying?	28
wished that she had attended a course of formal lessons?	29
studied the language while she was waiting to do something else?	30

Language learning

A Laura

I was living with an English-speaking family and the idea was that I'd pick up a lot of language by being there with them, but it just wasn't happening. Everyone watched television all the time and rarely spoke to me, so I might as well have been at home watching the same channels on satellite TV. After a week I left and moved in with a couple who had young children, and that was much better. They were all very friendly and I could chat with them anytime, really. When I got things wrong they would often correct me and I think that helped me improve my speaking a lot. They didn't know much about grammar, though, so it was probably a mistake not to go to a language school every day and actually be taught it. I would also have liked to be nearer the city centre, because the house was so far out of town that I couldn't get to the kinds of places where other teenagers went in the evenings. Although often I was so tired after playing with the kids I was happy just to have an early night.

B Chloe

I really want to learn Polish so I bought a course of language lessons as an MP3 to play on my iPod. That meant I could work on it anywhere I went, particularly at those times when you've got nothing to do, like standing at the bus stop, or in cinema queues. Once I was concentrating so hard on getting a grammar point right that I completely forgot I was on the bus and I started repeating restaurant phrases aloud. I felt a bit uncomfortable when I noticed everyone looking at me, so I didn't do that again. Actually, one problem with learning on my own was not knowing when I was saying words properly and when I wasn't. I could have done with someone to correct me, really. I don't mean a teacher, just somebody who spoke Polish well. Overall, though, it was a useful course and I think it was good value for money. After I'd finished the beginner's level I bought the intermediate level and I'm on that now.

C Amy

I used the Internet to improve my Spanish. It wasn't the first time I'd tried this, but I enjoyed it much more this time, probably because I'm in my mid-teens now. It cost nothing, of course, and although at first I didn't know quite where to look, in the end I came across some great websites where I could practise reading and listening and do grammar exercises. At the same time, I was joining social networking sites like MySpace and getting in touch with Spanish-speaking teenagers from various parts of the world. I was careful, though, not to give out my personal details because when you're online you can never be quite sure who is contacting you, whatever the language is. I also tried online chat in Spanish, but I couldn't keep up with people. All the time I was thinking about my grammar and it was taking me so long to reply to each sentence after I'd read it that I didn't think it was fair on them, so I gave up. I'll try again sometime, though.

D Stacey

I had lessons in Hindi at a local language school. Our teacher was great and I really liked the book we were using, too, but unfortunately the only class available at my level was late in the evening. So after a long day at school, and then all the written homework we have to do, I didn't have a lot of energy left for language learning. Also, some of my classmates were much older than me and I didn't really get to know them. But that didn't matter because whenever we did group activities, which I'd never done before, but took to straight away, I made sure I was with the younger ones. I was having lessons every evening and that was costing my parents quite a lot, but we'd booked to go to India later that year so there was no time to lose. It was really important to me that I could communicate with people there in their own language.

Test 3 — PAPER 2 Writing Part 1

You **must** answer this question. Write your answer in **120–150** words in an appropriate style.

---

1 You have received an email from your English-speaking friend, Kay, who is thinking of buying items over the Internet. Read Kay's email and the notes you have made. Then write an email to Kay, using **all** your notes.

---

email

From: Kay Simmonds
Sent: 9th February
Subject: Online shopping

I know you've had some experience buying things over the Internet and I'm wondering if you still think it's a good idea. — *Yes, because …*

Suggest … — What are the best kinds of thing to buy that way? My friend Mark says it's easy to find good books and CDs online, but I'd be interested to know what you think.

Also, I'm not really sure about how I would pay for things. Should I send cash through the post? — *No, because …*

Explain — One last thing: if I buy something and it's not what I wanted, or it gets damaged in the post, what can I do?

Please email me back soon. I want to get started as soon as possible!

Love

Kay

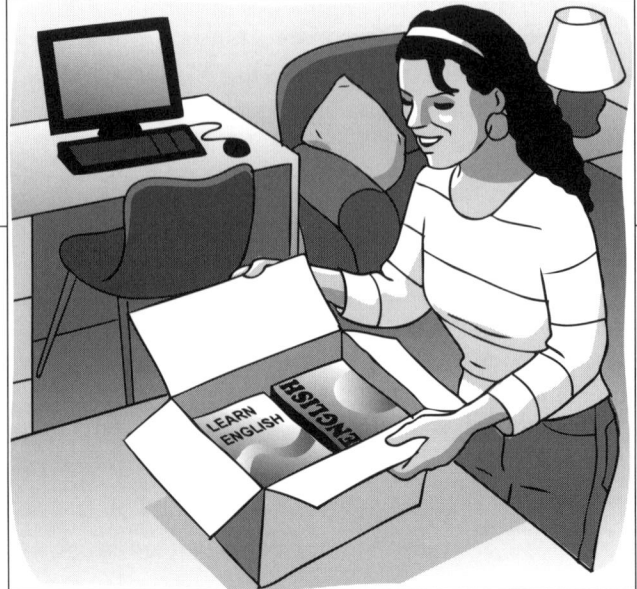

Write your **email**. You must use grammatically correct sentences with accurate spelling and punctuation in a style appropriate for the situation.

Test 3 — Writing Part 2

Write an answer to **one** of the questions **2–5** in this part. Write your answer in **120–180** words in an appropriate style.

2   Your English teacher has asked you to write a short **story** for the school magazine. The story must **begin** with the following words.

   When I look back on it now, I realise it was the most exciting day of my life.

   Write your **story**.

3   You recently saw this notice in *Internet Today* magazine.

   > A website that compares computer games is looking for reviews with the following title:
   > ***The last computer game I played.***

   You decide to write a **review** for the magazine. Describe the game and give your opinion of it. Would you recommend other people play it?

   Write your **review**.

4   You have had a discussion in your class about climate change. Your English teacher has now asked you to write an **essay**, giving your opinion on the following statement.

   We cannot prevent the Earth's climate from changing.

   Write your **essay**.

5   Answer **one** of the following two questions based on **one** of the titles below. Write the letter **(a)** or **(b)** as well as the number **5** in the question box.

   (a) [author/name of book]

   The story includes a number of events in which somebody is in danger. Your English teacher has asked the class to write an **article** describing one of these events and saying how the person deals with it.

   Write your **article**.

   (b) [author/name of book]

   An English-language magazine has asked readers to write a **report** on who could play the two main characters in a new film or TV version of the book. Say which well-known actors would be best suited to play each role, giving reasons in each case.

   Write your **report**.

Test 3

PAPER 3 Use of English Part 1

For questions **1–12**, read the text below and decide which answer (**A, B, C** or **D**) best fits each gap. There is an example at the beginning (**0**).

Mark your answers **on the separate answer sheet**.

Example:

0   **A** common   **B** frequent   **C** general   **D** routine

| 0 | A ▬ | B ▭ | C ▭ | D ▭ |

The sticking plaster

Nowadays, one of the most **(0)** ..... items found in the home is the sticking plaster.

Protecting a cut by covering the affected area with a piece of material that sticks to the skin may seem a rather **(1)** ..... idea, so it is perhaps surprising to learn that the plaster was not **(2)** ..... until about ninety years ago.

The person who thought **(3)** ..... the idea was Earle Dickson, an employee of the Johnson & Johnson company. Concerned that his wife Josephine sometimes **(4)** ..... accidents while cooking and doing other jobs, he used pieces of cotton material placed inside strips of sticky tape to cover her injuries. This prevented dirt getting into the **(5)** ..... and protected it from further harm as she did the **(6)** ..... .

Dickson's boss was impressed, so in 1921 Johnson & Johnson put the new sticking plaster into **(7)** ..... under the brand name Band-Aid. Sales at first were slow, but somebody at the company came up with the **(8)** ..... idea of giving free plasters to the Boy Scouts. This created publicity and from then **(9)** ..... it became a commercial success. Dickson was **(10)** ..... within the company, eventually becoming a senior executive.

Although the basic design of the sticking plaster has remained similar to the **(11)** ..... , there have been many developments in the materials used and it is now **(12)** ..... in a variety of shapes, sizes and colours. Total worldwide sales are believed to have exceeded 100 billion.

116 | Test 3

Use of English Part 1

1	A clear	B evident	C plain	D obvious
2	A realised	B imagined	C invented	D dreamt
3	A up	B over	C in	D forward
4	A did	B had	C made	D took
5	A wound	B damage	C breakage	D tear
6	A homework	B household	C housework	D homecoming
7	A creation	B formation	C production	D construction
8	A keen	B bright	C eager	D shining
9	A after	B to	C since	D on
10	A raised	B lifted	C advanced	D promoted
11	A model	B original	C sample	D standard
12	A available	B achievable	C accessible	D attainable

Test 3 — Use of English Part 2

For questions **13–24**, read the text below and think of the word which best fits each gap. Use only **one** word in each gap. There is an example at the beginning (**0**).

Write your answers **IN CAPITAL LETTERS** on the separate answer sheet.

Example: 0 | I N

Diving in the Red Sea

The Red Sea coast of Egypt is surely one of the best places **(0)** ...in... the world to go underwater diving. Its hot sunny climate and clear warm water make it the ideal place for beginners as **(13)** .... as for experienced divers, at any time of the year.

(14) .... over fifty diving centres in the area, many different types of diving are possible. At centres for complete beginners there are training courses **(15)** .... include simple dives with a qualified instructor. These dives **(16)** .... them used to being underwater and teach some basic skills **(17)** .... as swimming and breathing below the surface.

More experienced divers can choose **(18)** .... a vast range of possible activities and many of these can be enjoyed **(19)** .... as part of a group or, if they prefer, alone. Some like to explore the coast of the National Park, where the steep cliffs extend underwater to a depth **(20)** .... more than seventy metres. For dives of **(21)** .... kind it is advisable to be accompanied by a guide, on **(22)** .... of the strong currents which can suddenly change direction.

For really advanced divers, there are some fascinating wrecks at **(23)** .... bottom of the Red Sea. **(24)** .... visits to these old ships require quite long boat trips, it is well worth going just to see the huge variety of beautiful plants and fish down there.

Test 3 — Use of English Part 3

For questions **25–34**, read the text below. Use the word given in capitals at the end of some of the lines to form a word that fits in the gap **in the same line**. There is an example at the beginning (**0**).

Write your answers **IN CAPITAL LETTERS** on the separate answer sheet.

Example: **0** S U R P R I S I N G L Y

Hot-air balloons

Riding in a hot-air balloon is a (0) *surprisingly* calm and peaceful experience, quite (25) .... any other form of flying. With no engines to provide power, a balloon depends (26) .... on the winds around it to move in any direction. (27) .... , the maximum speed is normally around 15 kilometres per hour.

SURPRISE
LIKE
ENTIRE
CONSEQUENCE

This kind of balloon is based on the simple (28) .... principle that the (29) .... of hot air is less than that of cold air. It is not, however, a large (30) .... , as a cubic metre of hot air is only about 250 grams lighter than the same amount of cold air. This means it takes (31) .... four cubic metres of hot air just to lift one kilo, which explains why balloons that carry people have to be so enormous.

SCIENCE
WEIGH
DIFFERENT

ROUGH

A gas burner is used to (32) .... the air inside the balloon, causing it to rise. To go up more slowly, or to make a (33) .... , hot air is released from the top of the balloon. The fact that the wind blows in different directions at different heights (34) .... the pilot to steer the balloon left or right by moving it to higher or lower positions in the sky.

HOT
DESCEND

ABLE

Test 3 — Use of English Part 4

For questions **35–42**, complete the second sentence so that it has a similar meaning to the first sentence, using the word given. **Do not change the word given**. You must use between **two** and **five** words, including the word given. Here is an example (**0**).

0   Travelling by car is becoming increasingly expensive.

   GETTING

   Travelling by car .... expensive.

The gap can be filled by the words 'is getting more', so you write:

Example: | 0 | IS GETTING MORE |

Write **only** the missing words **IN CAPITAL LETTERS on the separate answer sheet**.

---

35   I'm sure it was a surprise when you saw Jake at the party.

   BEEN

   You .... see Jake at the party.

36   This is a very dry part of the country.

   HARDLY

   In this part of the country .... rains.

37   In the morning I have a twenty-minute walk to school.

   TAKES

   In the morning .... to walk to school.

38   It was impossible for us to go to school because of the bus strike.

   PREVENTED

   The bus strike .... to school.

39   On hearing the fire alarm, you must leave the building as quickly as possible.

   SOON

   You must leave the building .... the fire alarm.

40   I am trying to study, so would you mind not making that noise?

   RATHER

   I am trying to study, so I .... make that noise.

41   Karen doesn't like to play the piano as much as I do.

   KEEN

   Karen .... playing the piano than I am.

42   'How are you feeling after your operation, Chloe?' the doctor asked.

   SHE

   The doctor asked .... after her operation.

Test 3 PAPER 4 Listening Part 1

03 You will hear people talking in eight different situations. For questions **1–8**, choose the best answer (**A**, **B** or **C**).

1 You hear an advertisement for a local taxi firm.
   Which aspect are they emphasising?

   A   low fares
   B   reliable service
   C   comfortable cars

2 You hear a radio phone-in programme about a plan to build a new supermarket.
   Why has the woman phoned?

   A   to protest about the building of the supermarket
   B   to demand that it should employ local staff only
   C   to support the plan if certain conditions are met

3 You hear a young woman talking about a concert by her favourite band.
   What aspect of the concert disappointed her?

   A   the length of the band's performance
   B   the quality of the sound there
   C   the distance she was from the stage

4 On the radio news, you hear a story about a missing dog.
   Where was the dog found?

   A   in a street in town
   B   in the countryside
   C   in a town-centre park

5 In a radio play, you hear a man talking to a woman.
   What is he doing?

   A   complaining about something
   B   requesting something
   C   promising to do something

6 You overhear two people coming out of a football stadium.
   What does the man think?

   A   The referee was unfair.
   B   The match was boring.
   C   The better team won.

7 You hear a young woman talking about her favourite free-time activity.
   What is it?

   A   walking in the hills
   B   playing tennis
   C   going swimming

8 You overhear a man talking in an airport.
   Who is he?

   A   a passenger
   B   a flight attendant
   C   a taxi driver

Listening Part 1

Test 3 — Listening Part 2

04) You will hear part of a talk by a biologist called Jonas Hahn about carrots. For questions **9–18**, complete the sentences.

The magnificent carrot

The carrot is the _____**9**_____ most popular vegetable in the world.

Nowadays, _____**10**_____ produces more carrots than any other country.

Carrots were first grown _____**11**_____ ago, in Afghanistan.

Thousands of years ago, most cultivated carrots were _____**12**_____ not orange.

The carrot used to be regarded as _____**13**_____ rather than something to eat.

Dutch _____**14**_____ of the 16th century show orange carrots.

Carrots grown in _____**15**_____ soil are less bright in colour.

Jonas says that carrots are better for you if you _____**16**_____ them.

Eating carrots can help prevent the _____**17**_____ harming you.

In ten years' time, it may be possible to use carrots as _____**18**_____.

Test 3 — Listening Part 3

05 You will hear five different people talking about airports they have recently been to. For questions **19–23**, choose from the list (**A–F**) what each speaker says. Use the letters only once. There is one extra letter which you do not need to use.

A   We could see lots of planes taking off.

B   It took a long time to get through security.

C   Public transport to the airport was poor.

D   Our children enjoyed the play area.

E   I didn't have to pay to go on the Internet.

F   The airport was badly organised.

Speaker 1   19

Speaker 2   20

Speaker 3   21

Speaker 4   22

Speaker 5   23

Test 3 — Listening Part 4

🎧 06 You will hear an interview with Ryan Mackenzie, who works in a 15th-century castle. For questions **24–30**, choose the best answer (**A**, **B** or **C**).

24 What is Ryan's main task early in the morning?
 A to give instructions to other members of staff
 B to check the building has been properly cleaned
 C to find out what his boss wants him to do

25 During the day, his most important duty is
 A to check that everything is working properly.
 B to ensure the safety of visitors to the castle.
 C to make sure that nobody steals anything.

26 He believes that employees at the castle must be
 A experts in history.
 B retired police officers.
 C physically fit.

27 What does Ryan say about his uniform?
 A It looks ridiculous in the 21st century.
 B It had to be specially made for him.
 C It reflects the history of the castle.

28 What happened in the castle one night?
 A There was a fire in one of the rooms.
 B Some visitors were trapped inside.
 C Two people tried to steal a painting.

29 Ryan likes working at the castle because
 A there's always something new to learn.
 B the other staff are always cheerful.
 C it never gets cold inside the building.

30 How does he feel about living in Frankby village?
 A He says it's too close to where he works.
 B He feels that he's lucky to live there.
 C He thinks that it's a rather boring place.

Test 3 — PAPER 5 Speaking Parts 1 and 2

Part 1

3 minutes (5 minutes for groups of three)

Interlocutor First of all, we'd like to know something about you.

- Where are you from? What do you like about living there?
- What kind of food do you like most? Why?
- Tell us about the best holiday you've ever had.
- What do you think would be the perfect job for you? Why?

Part 2

4 minutes (6 minutes for groups of three)

Interlocutor In this part of the test, I'm going to give each of you two photographs. I'd like you to talk about your photographs on your own for about a minute, and also to answer a short question about your partner's photographs.

(Candidate A), it's your turn first. Here are your photographs on page C12 of the Speaking appendix (Task 1). They show **people watching different kinds of television programme**.

I'd like you to compare the photographs, and say **why you think people enjoy watching these kinds of programme**.

All right?

Candidate A

1 minute ....

Interlocutor Thank you.

(Candidate B), **which of these programmes would you rather watch?**

Candidate B

approximately 20 seconds ....

Interlocutor Thank you.

Now, *(Candidate B)*, here are your photographs on page C13 of the Speaking appendix (Task 2). **They show people buying clothes in different places**.

I'd like you to compare the photographs, and say **why you think people buy clothes in places like these**.

All right?

Candidate B

1 minute ....

Interlocutor Thank you.

(Candidate A), **in which of these places would you prefer to buy clothes?**

Candidate A

approximately 20 seconds ....

Interlocutor Thank you.

Test 3 — Speaking Parts 3 and 4

Part 3

3 minutes (4 minutes for groups of three)

Interlocutor

Now, I'd like you to talk about something together for about three minutes.

I'd like you to imagine that someone is going on a long journey by train on their own. Here are some pictures of things they can do while they are travelling.

Show candidates pictures on page C14 of the Speaking appendix.

First, talk to each other about **how well each of these ideas could help people pass the time on a long journey.** Then decide **which two would be the most enjoyable.**

Part 4

4 minutes (5 minutes for groups of three)

Interlocutor

Select any of the following questions, as appropriate:

- How do you pass the time when you have to wait for a bus, train or plane?
- Which do you think is the most comfortable way to travel long distances: by rail, road or air? Why?
- Some people say we should avoid unnecessary travel in order to protect the environment. Do you agree? Why?/Why not?

Thank you. That is the end of the test.

> *Select any of the following questions, as appropriate:*
> - **What do you think?**
> - **Do you agree?**
> - **And you?**

Test 4

PAPER 1 Reading Part 1

You are going to read a magazine article about learning Chinese. For questions **1–8**, choose the answer (**A**, **B**, **C** or **D**) which you think fits best according to the text.

Mark your answers **on the separate answer sheet**.

A year in China

How a year in China's 'romantic city' helped Hannes Ortner learn Chinese.

In China, Dalian is known as the 'romantic city', and during my year studying Chinese at Dalian Foreign Language University, I certainly fell in love: the language is the key to a fascinating way of life, while the city itself is surrounded by green hills and the ocean, and overlooked by a marvellous castle that I always meant to visit while I was there.

Dalian is generally quite a new city, without the long cultural history of Beijing, and the skyscrapers that have appeared in recent years are evidence of China's position as the world's fastest-growing economy. The boom has seen the number of foreigners coming to the country to learn Chinese increase enormously, and I was thankful that relatively few Westerners have discovered Dalian. I rarely had the opportunity to use Chinese in everyday situations in China's bigger cities, where European tourists are everywhere and young people are keen to practise their English.

I was the only Westerner in my class. After a four-hour oral exam and a written test, I was placed in a post-intermediate group with 12 people – all Asians. I was already three years into a four-year degree in Chinese culture and language, but it was still difficult to keep up with the Japanese and Korean students, who were much more familiar with Chinese characters (the symbols used in the written language). One of the big disadvantages at the University of Vienna had been the large classes, with 30–40 people trying to learn Chinese in just four hours a week. In Dalian we were taught five days a week for three hours plus another four hours one afternoon a week. Some of the older teachers still used traditional teaching methods, concentrating on reading texts, listening to tapes and learning by oral repetition, and although it initially took me a while to become accustomed to this, it really helped us improve our skills.

We had three teachers but Mrs Lin soon became our favourite. I was fortunate enough to have six weeks of additional classes with this wonderful lady after I was chosen to take part in the Dalian Chinese speech competition. In preparation for the event, we met for two hours a day to work on my pronunciation using a text she had written called 'I love Dalian'. I found the whole experience quite demanding – from the intense training to speaking in front of a large audience (including Chinese teachers) – but it was the best language training I have ever received and I thank my patient teachers for the fact that I eventually won the competition. It was this experience that made me determined to perfect my command of the language.

Chinese is sometimes said to be one of the most difficult languages to learn, mainly because of its complex grammar, writing system (which uses a vast number of characters) and system of tones (every syllable in standard Chinese can be pronounced in four different ways depending on meaning). But Mrs Lin knew how to explain things in a simple way and, with her as my teacher, I realised that Chinese does not deserve its reputation for difficulty.

The second term had already started when I decided to move out of my Western-style flat and into a more traditional Chinese one, and I had to fill out a number of official documents. For Westerners in China, moving house involves re-registering at the police station and a certain amount of form-filling. On several occasions I had to bite my lip and remember that young Asian people coming to the West to study would probably have to go through a similar procedure, but in the end I was able to move into my new place.

During that second term I got my head down and concentrated on improving my language skills before returning to Austria to finish my degree. I adore China – its magnificent landscapes, its people with their unique history and, above all, its language, which introduced me to a new way of thinking and a rich cultural history, and ultimately helped me broaden my horizons.

1 Apart from the natural beauty of Dalian, why did the writer enjoy staying there?
   A It has always been an important centre of Chinese culture.
   B Near the city there is an old building that he often visited.
   C While he was there he was in love with another student.
   D His studies enabled him to understand Chinese society.

2 Why did he prefer Dalian to other Chinese cities?
   A He didn't have to speak in Chinese all the time.
   B There were not so many people from the West.
   C He could help local people learn to speak English.
   D He had always liked seeing modern buildings.

3 What does the writer say about his lessons at Dalian University?
   A The number of students in the class was far too high.
   B He should have been placed in a much lower-level class.
   C Some of his classmates made faster progress than him.
   D Students did not spend enough time in the classroom.

4 How did he feel about the way he was taught Chinese in Dalian?
   A It was impossible for him to get used to it.
   B It was a pity he only did reading and listening.
   C It was different but it was highly effective.
   D It was not as good as the teaching in Vienna.

5 What change occurred as a result of his involvement in the speech competition?
   A He felt he did not need to continue improving his Chinese.
   B He had extra lessons with the teacher he admired most.
   C He began to write his own texts in Chinese about Dalian.
   D He no longer found it difficult to make speeches in Chinese.

6 What did he discover about the Chinese language?
   A Some aspects of the grammar are very simple.
   B It is easier to learn than some people claim.
   C The pronunciation of short words is easy to learn.
   D It is impossible for Westerners to learn it outside China.

7 What is meant by 'bite my lip' in line 62?
   A stop myself saying something
   B smile at what somebody said
   C say something that wasn't true
   D get very angry with somebody

8 What conclusion does the writer draw about his stay in China?
   A It was enjoyable being there but he was glad to return to Europe.
   B The thing he loved most was seeing the beautiful scenery there.
   C Learning Chinese made him interested in a wider range of things.
   D He would never really understand the way people there think.

Test 4 — Reading Part 2

You are going to read an article about blogs (the internet sites where individuals regularly write their own thoughts and comments). Seven sentences have been removed from the article. Choose from the sentences **A–H** the one which fits each gap (**9–15**). There is one extra sentence which you do not need to use.

Get blogging!

Do you want others to read what you write online? Try setting up a blog with Susan Purcell's guide to getting started.

Short for 'weblogs', blogs began as online diaries, but these days many are useful and entertaining sources of news and information. A blog is really a kind of mini-website, but with one big difference: it costs nothing, or very little, to run. What makes blogs different from most websites is that they are updated regularly and they are interactive – readers can comment on what you write.

9 ☐ You type your text as if it were any article and the software of the blog company does the rest. Each time you add another piece of text, known as a 'post', that gets published at the top of the page and everything else moves down.

More than 130 million blogs have been started on the web and around a million blog posts are written every day. Every blog is different: some have only one author, some are the work of two or more people, some are streams of nonsense about nothing in particular. **10** ☐ These are often the ones that attract most comments.

People blog for different reasons. Some blogs are platforms for the writers' own opinions, some bloggers write to promote themselves and show off their skills, some even sell stuff on their blogs. Other bloggers write to get in touch with people who have similar views, while some blog to share their knowledge. **11** ☐ Blogs can be password-protected so that they can only be read by those who are allowed to view them.

The best blogs are those that specialise. If you cover too wide a topic area, you'll find it difficult to attract a loyal audience. People go to their favourite blog regularly, as they know they'll always find something of interest there. **12** ☐ You'll come across as knowledgeable and others with the same interest will visit regularly.

It is very easy to set up a blog. You can be online within a few minutes of opening an account. Start by looking at as many blogs as possible to get ideas. Most blogs publish a 'blogroll', or list of links to other blogs, so click on those to view more examples. **13** ☐ The biggest and most user-friendly are free, although they all offer slightly different features, so make sure you investigate and choose the one that provides what you want.

You can write as much or as little as you like but you must add posts regularly. It is best to write every few days, but it doesn't matter if you do so only at weekends or a couple of times a month, so long as your readers know when to expect posts. It is frustrating to visit a favourite blog only to find that it hasn't been updated as expected. You won't always have the time to write long blogs. **14** ☐

Blogging about items in the news will help increase your readership, as more people will be searching for that topic. **15** ☐ It is often more satisfying to attract regular readers who interact with you, so write about what you know, check your facts and don't be afraid to say things people may disagree with – it's a good way of attracting comments. You'll soon have a loyal audience who will spread the word about your blog.

- **A** On those days, refer your visitors to another blog, something in the press or a video clip on the Internet.
- **B** Many, though, are clever, informative and well written.
- **C** When you've done this, you'll be asked to choose a name for your blog, so have something ready.
- **D** They don't want a wasted visit, so stick to your own particular subject.
- **E** No technical knowledge is required to blog.
- **F** However, blogging is not necessarily about gaining a wide audience.
- **G** Teachers, for instance, often blog to help students to catch up when they miss a class.
- **H** Next you need to select a blog company.

Test 4 — Reading Part 3

You are going to read a magazine article about people who bought clothes in different ways. For questions **16–30**, choose from the people (**A–D**). The people may be chosen more than once. When more than one answer is required, these may be given in any order.

Mark your answers **on the separate answer sheet**.

Which person

was pleased with a replacement item?	16	
regretted not buying a different kind of item?	17	
was disappointed with the item after they had owned it for some time?	18	
had difficulty deciding which to buy as there were so many attractive items?	19	
became impatient while waiting to pay for the item?	20	
is sure they got a bargain?	21	22
had not previously bought clothes that way?	23	
had difficulty finding the right item because of the labelling?	24	
bought an item that was the wrong size?	25	
asked the seller a question about the item before they bought it?	26	
says they will always buy clothes in the same place?	27	
had not intended to buy clothes there?	28	
was in the street when they saw the item advertised?	29	
wished they had bought more than one of the same item?	30	

Shopping for clothes

A Brad Stevens

I was food shopping in the big supermarket near here and I saw they were selling jeans at a ridiculously low price, so I thought I'd pick up a pair. Later when I remembered I had a job interview the week after, I realised I should have bought some formal trousers instead, but I suppose it was just one of those things you suddenly do when you see something going cheap. Even though I probably could have got them for less on eBay. Anyway, I spent quite a bit of time going through this great pile of jeans because all the different sizes were mixed up and they weren't very clearly marked 'large' or 'extra large' or whatever. Eventually I came across a pair that seemed about my size and headed for the checkout. It was very slow there, and I got fed up standing in a line of about ten customers. Why they don't open more checkouts at busy times I really don't know.

B Sara Desai

I saw a stall selling sweaters when I was wandering around my usual clothes market and there was such a wide range of lovely ones that I was spoilt for choice. In the end I made my mind up and I enquired whether they had a particularly attractive pale blue one in medium. The stall holder said they had. I couldn't try it on there and then but I was sure it would fit me, so I paid and took it home. There I discovered that the sleeves were far too short so I had to take it back. That was annoying, but the man on the stall quickly found me a larger one for the same very reasonable price and that turned out to be just right on me. I'd wasted an hour or so travelling to and from the market, but I still wouldn't dream of shopping for things like that anywhere else.

C Tania Ferreira

I was walking along the pavement looking for something new to wear when a sign in a shop window saying 'cotton jackets 50% off' caught my eye, so I went in. They didn't have one in my size but said they could order it for me. A few days later they called me to say it'd arrived and I went back to the shop to collect it. It fitted me perfectly, but when I tried it on, I just didn't take to the colour, a kind of grey-brown, and I said I'd prefer a lighter one. Again I had to wait, and again I went back to the shop. This time everything seemed fine, and I paid for it and took it home. After I'd worn it twice, though, I put it through the washing machine and was most upset to find it'd shrunk, despite the fact that I'd followed the washing instructions exactly. It was a waste of money, really.

D Ali Haddad

I'd picked up lots of things like books and computer games online, but that was the first time I'd actually got myself something to wear over the Internet. It looked like a really lovely shirt and the price was incredibly low, so I clicked on 'Buy it now', paid by credit card and waited for it to arrive. I thought afterwards that perhaps I should have emailed the seller to check the colour, because although it looked fine in the photo, it might not be exactly what I wanted. In the event I needn't have worried, and I was absolutely delighted when I saw it. I would have got another one if I'd known how good it would look.

Test 4

PAPER 2 Writing Part 1

You **must** answer this question. Write your answer in **120–150** words in an appropriate style.

1. You have received this letter from your English-speaking friend, Ronnie. Read Ronnie's letter and the notes you have made. Then write a letter to Ronnie, using **all** your notes.

I've just been talking to my mum and dad about our summer holidays, and they suggested that this year you could spend a couple of weeks with us! We stay right by the sea, the weather's always beautiful and there's plenty to do in the town. What do you think? — **Sounds great!**

We'll be there all summer, so if you can come, which month would suit you better: July or August? — **Say which, and why**

We have a small spare room in our apartment there and you'd be welcome to use that, or else you could stay at my elder sister's studio next door, as she's away studying in New Zealand. Which would you prefer? — **Tell Ronnie**

No, suggest ... — *Do you think you'd want to spend a lot of time on the beach? We could do other things too, like sports, or visiting places near there.*

Hope to hear from you soon!

Ronnie

Write your **letter**. You must use grammatically correct sentences with accurate spelling and punctuation in a style appropriate for the situation.

Test 4 — Writing Part 2

Write an answer to **one** of the questions **2–5** in this part. Write your answer in **120–180** words in an appropriate style.

---

2 You have had a discussion in your English class about computer games. Now your teacher has asked you to write an **essay**, giving your opinion on the following statement.

Playing computer games is a waste of time.

Write your **essay**.

3 You see this announcement on a website that publishes humorous stories.

> **The funniest thing I have ever seen.**
>
> Write and tell us what happened, where and when, and say why you found it so amusing.
>
> We will publish the best article on our site.

Write your **article**.

4 Here is part of a letter you have received from an English-speaking friend.

> *I'm thinking of visiting your country in the summer holidays and I'd like some advice. Which places do you recommend I go to, and what can I do there? I also want to see you, of course! When and where can we meet?*
>
> *Alex*

Write to your friend giving your advice and making some suggestions.

Write your **letter**.

5 Answer **one** of the following two questions based on **one** of the titles below. Write the letter **(a)** or **(b)** as well as the number **5** in the question box.

(a) [author/name of book]

An international magazine has asked for reviews of books that may be of interest to people of your age. Write a **review** of the book, outlining the story, saying what you liked or disliked about the book, and whether you would recommend it to other readers.

(b) [author/name of book]

Read this part of a letter from Megan, your English-speaking friend.

Write a **letter** to Megan, giving your opinion.

> *I love books that make me want to keep reading all day! Is the book you've just read exciting? Write and tell me what you think.*

Test 4 — PAPER 3 Use of English Part 1

For questions **1–12**, read the text below and decide which answer (**A, B, C** or **D**) best fits each gap. There is an example at the beginning (**0**).

Mark your answers **on the separate answer sheet**.

Example:

0   **A** far   **B** then   **C** back   **D** past

| 0 | A ▢ | B ▢ | C ▬ | D ▢ |

The joy of picnics

Years ago, **(0)** ..... in the days when I was just a kid, my family used to have Sunday picnics together in a **(1)** ..... part of the countryside. We would find a suitably quiet and pleasant **(2)** ..... , then spend several hours chatting, eating and playing games in the **(3)** ..... air. Since then, though, my parents' life has become so much busier and they never seem to have the time for **(4)** ..... family meals any more.

In my **(5)** ..... this is a great pity, so I've recently started to organise picnics of my **(6)** .... I get in touch with some of my closest friends and first we **(7)** ..... on a suitable place to go. Then we talk about who'll bring which food. This **(8)** ..... that there will be a variety of tasty things to eat, particularly **(9)** ..... everyone makes the meals they do best. It's important, though, to keep the food simple, as everything has to **(10)** ..... into a backpack and then be carried across fields and up river valleys.

When we finally **(11)** ..... our destination, it's time to sit down, relax and enjoy each other's company. And I'm **(12)** ..... certain that food tastes far better on a picnic than anywhere else!

1 A close   B nearby   C near   D next
2 A spot   B point   C tip   D dot
3 A free   B empty   C wide   D open
4 A outer   B outdoor   C outward   D outgoing
5 A view   B regard   C thought   D belief
6 A self   B part   C behalf   D own
7 A decide   B determine   C fix   D arrange
8 A assures   B insures   C ensures   D secures
9 A unless   B so   C if   D though
10 A fit   B match   C suit   D join
11 A arrive   B get   C achieve   D reach
12 A remarkably   B absolutely   C extremely   D highly

Test 4 — Use of English Part 2

For questions **13–24**, read the text below and think of the word which best fits each gap. Use only **one** word in each gap. There is an example at the beginning (**0**).

Write your answers **IN CAPITAL LETTERS on the separate answer sheet**.

Example: **0** G O

Safe camping

Camping in the countryside is usually great fun, but sometimes things can **(0)** ...*go*... wrong. Accidents can happen, **(13)** .... it is essential to think about safety both before you go and while you are there. This will prevent your fun camping trip turning **(14)** .... something less pleasant.

Firstly, you need to plan ahead. Check out the weather forecast a few days **(15)** .... advance and watch out for any reports of fires in the area you are thinking **(16)** .... going to. Prepare an emergency kit in **(17)** .... you or anyone with you has an accident or illness while you are there.

Choose your campsite carefully, avoiding any places **(18)** .... there is a risk of flooding. Before you put up your tent, make **(19)** .... there are no sharp objects on the ground, or ants' or wasps' nests nearby.

In **(20)** .... to keep insects out of the tent, close it whenever you go in or out. If you need a camp fire for cooking, be careful **(21)** .... to build it anywhere near your tent, and before you go to bed, remember to put it **(22)** .... completely, preferably with lots of water.

After meals, pick up any bits of food that **(23)** .... be left on the ground, as these can attract insects – or larger creatures. It also makes sense, for **(24)** .... same reason, to keep unused food in closed containers well away from the camp. You don't want a hungry bear or other animal suddenly appearing in your tent!

Test 4 — Use of English Part 3

For questions **25–34**, read the text below. Use the word given in capitals at the end of some of the lines to form a word that fits in the gap **in the same line**. There is an example at the beginning (**0**).

Write your answers **IN CAPITAL LETTERS** on the separate answer sheet.

Example: | 0 | H | I | S | T | O | R | I | A | N | S | | | | | | |

A brief history of surfing

Most (**0**) *historians* agree that surfing began centuries ago in the Hawaii **HISTORY**
Islands in the Pacific Ocean, where the (**25**) .... regarded it as an **INHABIT**
important part of their culture, not as a recreational (**26**) .... It **ACTIVE**
was not until the early 20th century that it achieved (**27**) .... as a **RECOGNISE**
sport, and for many years it remained (**28**) .... to see surfers **USUAL**
anywhere other than in three main (**29**) .... : Hawaii, California and **LOCATE**
Australia.

All that began to change in the 1960s, partly as a result of (**30**) .... **IMPROVE**
in the design of surfboards, but also because of the success of films
and pop bands, (**31**) .... The Beach Boys, that were associated with **PARTICULAR**
surfing culture. Since then there has been rapid (**32**) .... in the **GROW**
popularity of surfing throughout the world, and for many surfers it
has become a highly (**33**) .... sport that requires skill and courage **COMPETE**
to deal with the (**34**) .... conditions in some of the roughest seas on **CHALLENGE**
Earth.

Test 4 — Use of English Part 4

For questions **35–42**, complete the second sentence so that it has a similar meaning to the first sentence, using the word given. **Do not change the word given**. You must use between **two** and **five** words, including the word given. Here is an example (0).

0 I first met Louis a year ago.

   YEAR

   It .... I first met Louis.

The gap can be filled by the words 'is a year since', so you write:

Example: | 0 | IS A YEAR SINCE |

Write **only** the missing words **IN CAPITAL LETTERS on the separate answer sheet**.

---

35 This time I didn't manage to win first prize.

   SUCCEED

   I didn't .... first prize this time.

36 Last night the theatre was almost empty.

   ANYBODY

   Last night .... the theatre.

37 My elder sister likes to look after small children.

   CARE

   My elder sister enjoys .... small children.

38 I've never heard such a silly story!

   SILLIEST

   That story is .... heard!

39 Amy asked what my reaction to her decision was.

   FELT

   Amy asked .... her decision.

40 The meeting probably won't last more than a few minutes.

   UNLIKELY

   The meeting .... on for more than a few minutes.

41 It's possible that Linda didn't take the early train.

   MIGHT

   Linda .... the early train.

42 It was raining heavily so I stayed at home.

   IF

   I would have gone out .... raining heavily.

Test 4   PAPER 4 Listening Part 1

07 You will hear people talking in eight different situations. For questions **1–8**, choose the best answer (**A**, **B** or **C**).

1 You hear a man talking on the radio about a special kind of computer mouse.
  How does this mouse differ from others?

  A   It can help people avoid injury.
  B   It is cheaper than a standard mouse.
  C   It changes what's on the screen faster.

2 You switch on the radio and hear a woman talking.
  Why did she decide to go abroad?

  A   to help people in another country
  B   to make money by working hard
  C   to spend several months as a tourist

3 You overhear a man talking to a colleague about a company training course.
  What is the man's opinion of the course?

  A   It was difficult to understand.
  B   It was a waste of time.
  C   It didn't last long enough.

4 You hear two people talking.
  Where are they?

  A   at an airport
  B   at a bus stop
  C   at a railway station

5 You hear a young man talking about moving to a big city.
  What was his biggest problem there?

  A   making new friends
  B   not having enough money
  C   having to live on his own

6 You overhear a woman talking on the phone about an airport expansion plan.
  What is she most worried about?

  A   more frequent noise
  B   longer traffic jams
  C   increased pollution

7 You overhear a man talking to a shop assistant about a DVD.
  What does he want?

  A   to have his money back
  B   to obtain a better copy of it
  C   to exchange it for something else

8 You overhear two people discussing holidays.
  Where did the woman go last month?

  A   Mexico
  B   the USA
  C   Canada

Test 4 — Listening Part 2

08) You will hear an interview with Vanessa Symons, who organises walking holidays for young people, on how best to pack a backpack. For questions **9–18**, complete the sentences.

Packing your bags

Packing a backpack well may prevent you losing _____ **9** when you walk.

Begin by making a _____ **10** of things to take.

Check the _____ **11** before deciding what clothes to take.

It is easy to carry _____ **12** clothes because they are fairly light.

Vanessa suggests taking _____ **13** of socks for a one-week trip.

Vanessa recommends putting food in _____ **14** when taking a backpack.

Vanessa suggests putting everything on the _____ **15** before you begin to pack.

Vanessa usually puts her _____ **16** into her backpack first.

Vanessa puts her hat in the _____ **17** part of her backpack.

When her backpack is full, Vanessa walks round a _____ **18** to test it.

Test 4 — Listening Part 3

09 You will hear five different people talking about things they were relieved about. For questions **19–23**, choose from the list (**A–F**) what each speaker says. Use the letters only once. There is one extra letter which you do not need to use.

A finding an object

B passing an exam

C seeing someone again

D escaping punishment

E winning a match

F avoiding injury

Speaker 1 — 19

Speaker 2 — 20

Speaker 3 — 21

Speaker 4 — 22

Speaker 5 — 23

Test 4 — Listening Part 4

You will hear an interview with Lily Francis about walking to the ancient city of Machu Picchu in Peru. For questions **24–30**, choose the best answer (**A, B** or **C**).

24 What was the main reason Lily wanted to go to Machu Picchu?
- A the historical importance of the place
- B the beautiful scenery surrounding the city
- C the physical challenge of getting there

25 Lily prepared for her journey through the mountains by
- A walking quite long distances every day.
- B spending time at heights over 4,000 metres.
- C camping out in cold, wet conditions.

26 She decided to do her walk in July because
- A there would probably be fewer people there then.
- B she had to take her summer holidays then.
- C the weather conditions are best for walking then.

27 What did she find toughest about her journey?
- A There was some extremely cold weather.
- B She had to carry a very heavy tent.
- C Sometimes it was difficult to walk.

28 What surprised her during her journey?
- A how bright the stars were at night
- B how easy it was to talk to the children
- C how big the birds in the sky were

29 According to Lily, what was the best moment on the journey?
- A seeing the mountain behind Machu Picchu
- B arriving at the ruins of Machu Picchu city
- C watching the sun go down over Machu Picchu

30 Next summer, Lily will probably be
- A in the Himalaya mountains.
- B on the Greenland icecap.
- C near the Australian coast.

Test 4 — PAPER 5 Speaking Parts 1 and 2

Part 1

3 minutes (5 minutes for groups of three)

Interlocutor First of all, we'd like to know something about you.

- Where are you from? What do you like about living there?
- Which is/was your favourite school subject? Why?
- Tell us about the town or village where you live.
- Which sport or hobby would you most like to try? Why?

Part 2

4 minutes (6 minutes for groups of three)

Interlocutor In this part of the test, I'm going to give each of you two photographs. I'd like you to talk about your photographs on your own for about a minute, and also to answer a short question about your partner's photographs.

(Candidate A), it's your turn first. Here are your photographs on page C15 of the Speaking appendix (Task 1). They show **people listening to music**.

I'd like you to compare the photographs, and say **why you think people choose to listen to music in these different ways**.

All right?

Candidate A
1 minute ....

Interlocutor Thank you.

(Candidate B), **how do you prefer to listen to music?**

Candidate B
approximately 20 seconds ....

Interlocutor Thank you.

Now, *(Candidate B)*, here are your photographs on page C16 of the Speaking appendix (Task 2). They show **animals in different situations.**

I'd like you to compare the photographs, and say **which way of life you think is better for the animals**.

All right?

Candidate B
1 minute ....

Interlocutor Thank you.

(Candidate A), **would you like to work with animals?**

Candidate A
approximately 20 seconds ....

Interlocutor Thank you.

Test 4 — Speaking Parts 3 and 4

Part 3

3 minutes (4 minutes for groups of three)

Interlocutor

Now, I'd like you to talk about something together for about three minutes.

Here are some pictures which show places that are often found in a town or city.

Show candidates pictures on page C17 of the Speaking appendix.

First, talk to each other about **how useful each of these places is**. Then decide **which you think would be the best one to live near**.

Part 4

4 minutes (5 minutes for groups of three)

Interlocutor

Select any of the following questions, as appropriate:

- **What kind of things can make a town or city exciting for young people?**
- **Would you prefer to live downtown, or in a quieter place? Why?**
- **Do you think the social problems of big cities are getting better, or worse? Why?**

Thank you. That is the end of the test.

> *Select any of the following questions, as appropriate:*
> - **What do you think?**
> - **Do you agree?**
> - **And you?**

PAPER 1 Reading Part 1

You are going to read an extract from a novel. For questions **1–8**, choose the answer (**A**, **B**, **C** or **D**) which you think fits best according to the text.

Mark your answers **on the separate answer sheet**.

Mma Ramotswe looked into her teacup. The red bush tea, freshly poured, was still very hot, too hot to drink, but good to look at in its amber darkness, and very good to smell. It was a pity, she thought, that she had become accustomed to the use of tea bags, as this meant that there were no leaves to be seen swirling around the surface or clinging to the side of the cup. She had given in on the issue of tea bags, out of weakness, she admitted; tea bags were so overwhelmingly more convenient than leaf tea, with its tendency to clog drains and the spouts of teapots too if one was not careful. She had never worried about getting the occasional tea leaf in her mouth, indeed she had rather enjoyed this, but that never happened now, with these neatly packed tea bags and their very precise, enmeshed doses of chopped leaves.

It was the first cup of the morning, as Mma Ramotswe did not count the two cups that she had at home before she came to work. One of these was consumed as she took her early stroll around the yard, with the sun just up, pausing to stand under the large acacia tree and peer up into the thorny branches above her, drawing the morning air into her lungs and savouring its freshness. That morning she had seen a chameleon on a branch of the tree and she had watched the strange creature fix its riveting eye upon her, its tiny prehensile feet poised in mid-movement. It was a great advantage, she thought, to have chameleon's eyes, which could look backwards and forwards independently. That would be a fine gift for a detective.

Now at her desk, she raised the cup to her lips and took a sip of the bush tea. She looked at her watch. Mma Makutsi was usually very punctual, but today she was late for some reason. This would be the fault of the minibuses, thought Mma Ramotswe. There would be enough of them coming into town from Tlokweng at that hour of the morning, but not enough going in the opposite direction. Mma Makutsi could walk, of course – her new house was not all that far away – but people did not like to walk in the heat, understandably enough.

She had a report to write, and she busied herself with this. It was not an easy one, as she had to detail the weaknesses she had found in the hiring department of a company which provided security guards. They imagined that they screened out applicants with a criminal record when they sought jobs with the company; Mma Ramotswe had discovered that it was simplicity itself to lie about one's past on the application form and that the forms were usually not even scrutinised by the official in charge of the personnel department. This man, who had got the job through lying about his qualifications and experience, rubber-stamped the applications of virtually anybody, but particularly the applications submitted by any of his relatives. Mma Ramotswe's report would not make comfortable reading for the company, and she knew to expect some anger over the results. This was inevitable – people did not like to be told uncomfortable truths, even if they had asked for them. Uncomfortable truths meant that one had to go back and invent a whole new set of procedures, and that was not always welcome when there were so many other things to do.

As she listed the defects in the firm's arrangements, Mma Ramotswe thought of how difficult it was to have a completely secure system for anything. The No. 1 Ladies' Detective Agency was a case in point. They kept all their records in two old filing cabinets, and neither of these, she realised, had a lock, or at least a lock that worked. There was a lock on the office door, naturally enough, but during the day they rarely bothered to use that if both of them went out on some errand.

1   What did Mma Ramotswe regret doing?

    A   drinking tea while it was too hot
    B   choosing tea of that colour
    C   changing the way she made tea
    D   making a cup of tea at that time

2   What did Mma Ramotswe feel was a problem with tea leaves?

    A   They often stuck to the tea cup.
    B   They got into her mouth.
    C   They could cause blockages.
    D   They floated in the tea.

3   Early every morning, Mma Ramotswe

    A   watched the sunrise from the yard.
    B   drank tea while she was in the yard.
    C   breathed in the hot air in the yard.
    D   left her office and went into the yard.

4   What is meant by 'a fine gift' in line 27?

    A   an excellent present
    B   a serious problem
    C   an ideal pet
    D   a useful ability

5   What did Mma Ramotswe think when Mma Makutsi did not arrive on time?

    A   Mma Makutsi should have walked to the office.
    B   Mma Makutsi was not to blame for being late.
    C   Mma Makutsi was late for work far too often.
    D   Mma Makutsi ought to live closer to the office.

6   What did Mma Ramotswe find out about an employee of the security firm?

    A   He frequently helped members of his family to get jobs.
    B   He had not told the company about his criminal record.
    C   He had told the truth in his own application form.
    D   He only approved applications from his own relatives.

7   How did Mma Ramotswe expect the firm to react to her report?

    A   They would feel it told them nothing new.
    B   They would ask her to write the whole report again.
    C   They would not be pleased by what it said.
    D   They would thank her for telling them the truth.

8   What does 'that' in line 66 refer to?

    A   the office door
    B   a filing cabinet
    C   a lock on the door
    D   a lock on a filing cabinet

Reading Part 1

Test 5 — Reading Part 2

You are going to read an article about ice-skating on a canal in Canada. Seven sentences have been removed from the article. Choose from the sentences **A–H** the one which fits each gap (**9–15**). There is one extra sentence which you do not need to use.

Skating on the Rideau Canal
by Susanne Pacher

Ottawa is known as one of the coldest capitals in the world, but it has turned a disadvantage into a major attraction and really shows us how to celebrate winter.

First there is Winterlude, Ottawa's winter festival, which is attended by more than 650,000 people and includes a whole range of events: concerts, fun activities, cooking demonstrations and many others. Then there is skating on the Rideau Skateway, recognised by the *Guinness Book of World Records* as the world's largest naturally frozen ice rink. The skating course is 7.8 kilometers long and takes you from the Rideau Bridge in the city centre all the way to Dow's Lake, and this was our main reason for coming to Ottawa.

Actually, we had travelled to Ottawa three years ago, but owing to warm weather, Winterlude was a big disappointment on that occasion. **9** My friend Theresa and I decided to come back this year, hoping for better weather so that we would be able to check out this fantastic skating and entertainment festival for ourselves.

We got going early at around 10 o'clock on an absolutely perfect winter morning. Even at that time there were already lots of people on the frozen canal, with a long queue in Confederation Park waiting to join them. We laced up our skates and put our boots in our backpacks. **10** Or, if we got too tired, we could even hop on the 'Snow-Bus' which connects Dow's Lake with Confederation Park during the entire festival for just $2.50.

In fact, we didn't need a Snow-Bus. **11** On this gorgeous day with crystal blue skies, perfect winter weather and no wind at all, going along the canal was a marvellous experience. We couldn't have picked a better day to explore it.

At intervals along the way there was a series of rest areas with entertainment and information centres. In many of them were the traditional Ottawa rows of stalls selling freshly-made hot cakes, covered with sugar. **12**

At the Concord Station Rest Area there was an exhibition on Ottawa's railroad history. Many years ago, apparently, trains would arrive in downtown Ottawa right next to the Rideau Canal. At Fifth Avenue, young sports fans were jumping through the air on a trampoline system and putting their hockey skills to the test.

When we arrived at Dow's Lake we watched the 26th Annual Bed Race, a fundraising event in which competing teams have to push a bed 50 metres along the ice. It made everyone laugh, and it was for a good cause, too. But we wanted to cover some more distance, so we started skating back towards downtown and by that time the course had filled up considerably. **13** Parents were pulling their children on little sleds, or even pushing them in all-terrain baby carriages. Everybody was having a lot of fun.

After all this skating we felt really hungry, so we took off our skates and headed for the Rideau Centre, one of Ottawa's biggest shopping centres. **14** The Rideau offered a welcome opportunity to warm up and catch a nice lunch in its café area.

I really love outdoor activities, as well as urban exploring. **15** I got a brief taste of this very special winter activity, and one thing is for sure: I'll be back!

A	That would enable us to get off the ice at any time and continue our explorations on foot.	F	Skating on the Rideau Canal through downtown Ottawa, therefore, combines both activities perfectly.
B	So we got on and went down the road that ran alongside the canal until we reached the lake.	G	It seemed as though the whole family, young and old, was out.
C	Our earlier experience, though, hadn't put us off.	H	Instead, we skated our way down on this wonderful natural ice surface all the way to the lake and didn't even need to rest.
D	It is located right next to the canal and was positively packed with people enjoying a good meal during the winter sales.		
E	They must surely be the perfect snack and energy source on a cold winter's day.		

Test 5 — Reading Part 3

You are going to read a magazine article about ways of reducing the environmental harm we do. For questions **16–30**, choose from the people (**A–D**). The people may be chosen more than once.

Mark your answers **on the separate answer sheet.**

Which person

avoids waste by selecting items carefully?	16
says other people have followed their example?	17
was ill for a short time?	18
believes the climate in their country has changed?	19
thinks that keeping things for long periods of time harms the environment?	20
sometimes forgets to do something that they feel they should do?	21
claims that they are healthier than other people?	22
found it quite easy to change their daily habits?	23
makes different choices according to the time of year?	24
has followed the advice of a colleague?	25
changed their original plans for environmental reasons?	26
sometimes feels physically uncomfortable because of a change they made?	27
says the damage to the environment is permanent?	28
agreed with the others they were with about what they should do first?	29
spent a lot more than they intended?	30

Saving the planet

A Carla

School student **Carla Ruiz** lives in a hot country and has become very aware of the need to save water. 'Spring and autumn used to be quite wet, but these days it hardly rains at all,' she says. 'Nearly all the rivers have dried up, destroying all the wildlife in and around them, and no matter what we do they'll never be the same again. At least, though, we can use what little water there is more sensibly. That's why at home I recently decided to do simple things like making sure there are no dripping taps, or taps left on while I'm brushing my teeth or washing food; also having showers instead of baths and not overwatering the plants. Within a few days I was regularly doing these things without even thinking, and I know they made a difference because the water bills went down quite a bit. My parents noticed that so they started doing the same, and our bills are now a lot lower.'

B Vincent

Trainee manager, **Vincent Owen**, is doing his bit to save the planet by using less electricity around the home. 'I was talking to this guy at work and he told me that we waste a huge amount of energy every year by leaving things like the TV, DVD and computer on standby all the time, so nowadays I try to remember – not always successfully – to switch them off at night. Something I always do now, though, is keep the air-conditioning off, even if I get a bit too sweaty here in summer. Incidentally, I've now got solar panels on the roof so that all the hot water is powered by the sun. That was a big investment, and it ended up well over budget, but I'm sure it'll pay for itself in the end. I was hoping the neighbours might go for solar energy too, but as yet there's no sign they will.'

C Lin

While **Lin Chen** is on a gap year, she is travelling round Europe with friends. 'We had intended to fly everywhere,' she says, 'but when we worked out just how much extra pollution that would cause, we decided to do it by train instead. It was cheaper, too.' They began their tour in Greece: 'We all felt the obvious place to start was where European civilisation began, so our first rail journey began in Athens. We travelled to Patras on the west coast, taking the ferry across to Bari in southern Italy. Unfortunately it was very windy and I had a bad case of sea-sickness, though, by the time we were on the train to Bologna, I'd recovered. From there we took the overnight train to Paris, and a few days later we went on the Eurostar to London. We saw far more of the countryside than we would have done by plane, and it was much more relaxing, too.'

D Tanya

Tanya Petrov works in a restaurant with an extensive menu, but at home she will only eat local or seasonal food: 'I strongly believe that transporting food thousands of kilometres, or storing it under refrigeration for months on end, ultimately has a highly negative impact on the climate. I always try to buy food that is produced locally, and I have a special calendar to show me which kinds of food are in season so that I know what I'm buying is really fresh. And I always check the "best-before" dates of fresh fruit and vegetables before I choose them so I don't end up having to throw any out. Apart from the environmental considerations, I'm convinced the food I eat, which has far fewer chemicals in it, helps me avoid the kind of illnesses that seem to be so common these days.'

Test 5 — PAPER 2 Writing Part 1

You **must** answer this question. Write your answer in **120–150** words in an appropriate style.

1 You have received an email from your English-speaking friend, Chris, who is planning to visit you. Read Chris's email and the notes you have made. Then write an email to Chris, using **all** your notes.

---

email

From:	Chris McFadden
Sent:	16th July
Subject:	Visit

I know we agreed that I would visit you during the first week in August, but would you mind if I came the week after instead? — *Better, actually, because …*

I'm really looking forward to seeing your country for the first time. What do you think I'll particularly like about it? — *Tell Chris*

August there is quite different from summer in my country, so what clothes do you think I should bring with me? — *Suggest …*

I'll fly to the main airport, of course, but from there what's the best way to get to where you live? — *Give directions*

Speak to you again soon,

Chris

Write your **email**. You must use grammatically correct sentences with accurate spelling and punctuation in a style appropriate for the situation.

Test 5 — Writing Part 2

Write an answer to **one** of the questions **2–5** in this part. Write your answer in **120–180** words in an appropriate style.

2 You have recently had a class discussion on the food we eat. Now your English teacher has asked you to write an **essay**, giving your opinion on the following statement.

Much of the food sold in supermarkets is not good for us.

Write your **essay**.

3 You have decided to enter a short story competition on an English-language website. The competition rules say that the story must **begin** with the following words.

It was late and Zoe had missed the last bus, so she decided to walk all the way home.

Write your **story**.

4 You see this advertisement in an English-language magazine.

Clothes shop staff wanted

We are looking for someone to work in our clothes shop at the airport during the summer months, when there are many visitors from abroad. The successful applicant needs

- good spoken English
- an interest in clothes, including modern fashions
- to be able to work long hours, including weekends

If you are interested, apply in writing to the manager, Mr Williamson, saying why you think you would be suitable for the work.

Write your **letter of application**.

5 Answer **one** of the following two questions based on **one** of the titles below. Write the letter **(a)** or **(b)** as well as the number **5** in the question box.

(a) [author/name of book]

This is part of a letter from your English-speaking friend, Jack, who has read the same book as you.

> *From the way this book describes society at the time, it's clear that most people's lives were much harder than they are today. Don't you agree?*

Write Jack a **letter**, giving your opinion.

(b) [author/name of book]

You have had a class discussion about the relationship between two of the characters in the book. Your English teacher has now given you this **essay** for homework.

In what ways does the relationship between the two main characters change during the story?

Write your **essay**.

Test 5 — PAPER 3 Use of English Part 1

For questions **1–12**, read the text below and decide which answer (**A, B, C** or **D**) best fits each gap. There is an example at the beginning (**0**).

Mark your answers **on the separate answer sheet**.

Example:

0   **A** noticed   **B** solved   **C** found   **D** saw

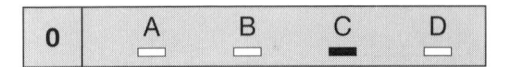

Email overload

A recent survey **(0)** ..... that office workers are suffering from an increasingly common 21st-century problem: too many emails. The study, which involved observing the **(1)** ..... of over 50 companies, appears to show that the huge number of messages they are now receiving is **(2)** ..... many of them from doing their jobs properly. In some cases, **(3)** ..... to the authors of the report, the negative **(4)** ..... on concentration can be as bad as losing a whole night's sleep.

The main problem seems to be that whenever employees receive emails, they feel **(5)** ..... to reply to them immediately. Often the message has nothing at all to **(6)** ..... with the work they are currently involved in, requiring them to focus on a completely different issue – until the next email arrives. These constant changes are tiring for the brain and this inevitably **(7)** ..... to poor overall performance.

Many employees continue to do this outside working **(8)** ....., checking their emails at home again and again just in **(9)** ..... there are any new messages. Some even do so while they are on holiday.

The solution, say the scientists who **(10)** ..... the survey, is relatively simple. Companies should advise people to check their emails far less often, possibly as **(11)** ..... as three or four times a day, reminding them that not every message needs an instant reply. They could also encourage their employees to relax more, and not **(12)** ..... their work quite so seriously.

1	**A** crew	**B** staff	**C** team	**D** band
2	**A** delaying	**B** opposing	**C** preventing	**D** interfering
3	**A** agreeing	**B** relating	**C** depending	**D** according
4	**A** effect	**B** result	**C** reaction	**D** product
5	**A** needed	**B** ordered	**C** commanded	**D** obliged
6	**A** see	**B** do	**C** make	**D** go
7	**A** results	**B** leads	**C** causes	**D** creates
8	**A** days	**B** terms	**C** hours	**D** turns
9	**A** case	**B** event	**C** time	**D** fact
10	**A** made up	**B** took part	**C** carried out	**D** filled in
11	**A** few	**B** many	**C** little	**D** much
12	**A** feel	**B** take	**C** think	**D** regard

Use of English Part 1

Test 5 — Use of English Part 2

For questions **13–24**, read the text below and think of the word which best fits each gap. Use only **one** word in each gap. There is an example at the beginning (**0**).

Write your answers **IN CAPITAL LETTERS** on the separate answer sheet.

Example: 0 | I N

Using mobile phones

Nowadays, just about everyone has a mobile phone. This wonderful invention enables people to stay **(0)** ..in.. touch with others at any time of day or night and no **(13)** .... where they are. It has brought people closer and it **(14)** .... certainly have saved many lives by enabling immediate contact with the emergency services.

It also, on the other **(15)** .... , has its disadvantages. Perhaps the most obvious of **(16)** .... is the sound of people talking loudly into their phone on public transport, apparently unaware **(17)** .... how much they are disturbing other travellers. This is now starting to happen even on aeroplanes, where until recently passengers **(18)** .... always told to keep their cell phones switched off.

Quite **(19)** .... from the annoyance they cause, those who shout into their phones in public **(20)** .... also be taking unnecessary risks. It is amazing **(21)** .... often people talk about highly personal subjects, including money matters, when they have no idea **(22)** .... might be listening to their every word.

Finally, there is the sound of other people's ringtones, all too often **(23)** .... maximum volume. The owner of the phone may think their choice of music is cool, but everyone around them probably just wishes they **(24)** .... turn it down – or off.

Test 5 — Use of English Part 3

For questions **25–34**, read the text below. Use the word given in capitals at the end of some of the lines to form a word that fits in the gap **in the same line**. There is an example at the beginning (**0**).

Write your answers **IN CAPITAL LETTERS** on the separate answer sheet.

Example: **0** A S S I S T A N C E

112 pets

A woman living in the city centre has asked for (**0**) *assistance* to find a bigger house and garden – so that her 112 pets can live in less (**25**) .... conditions. Jennifer Symons, 26, has always loved animals and now has a (**26**) .... that includes twelve cats, seven dogs, four monkeys, two horses and a (**27**) .... of smaller creatures, including hamsters, parrots and tropical fish.

ASSIST
CROWD
COLLECT
VARY

She also has a number of snakes, and although none of them, she says, is (**28**) .... , some of her neighbours in Lower Market Street remain (**29**) .... and are worried that they might escape. Generally, though, people seem to like Jennifer's pets and are always (**30**) .... towards her.

POISON
CONVINCE
FRIEND

All these animals, however, have to be looked after, and Jennifer has to get up at 5.30 every morning to start (**31**) .... some of them. Cleaning and other tasks take up so much time that taking care of them has now become almost her main (**32**) .... , leaving her with only her (**33**) .... from a part-time job at a local supermarket to maintain the 112 and herself. It is hardly (**34**) .... , therefore, that she can't really afford to move into a bigger house.

FOOD
OCCUPY
EARN
SURPRISE

Test 5 — Use of English Part 4

For questions **35–42**, complete the second sentence so that it has a similar meaning to the first sentence, using the word given. **Do not change the word given.** You must use between **two** and **five** words, including the word given. Here is an example (**0**).

0 You're still making too many mistakes in your written work, I'm afraid.

   THERE

   I'm afraid .... too many mistakes in your written work.

The gap can be filled by the words 'there are still', so you write:

Example: | 0 | THERE ARE STILL |

Write **only** the missing words **IN CAPITAL LETTERS on the separate answer sheet**.

---

35 They think the jewel thief is planning another crime.

   THOUGHT

   The jewel thief .... planning another crime.

36 'Can you lend me some money, Marta?' asked David.

   BORROW

   David asked Marta .... some money.

37 I saw the race begin because I arrived at the stadium on time.

   MISSED

   If I hadn't arrived at the stadium on time, I .... of the race.

38 I think you ought to decide right now.

   WERE

   If I .... a decision right now.

39 The rider of the stolen motorbike was a man aged about 25.

   RIDDEN

   The stolen motorbike .... a man aged about 25.

40 I'm sorry I went out last night.

   WISH

   I .... out last night.

41 If you don't work harder, you won't pass the exam.

   UNLESS

   You won't pass the exam .... work.

42 I really don't want to tidy my room right now.

   FEEL

   I really don't .... my room right now.

158 | Test 5

Test 5 — PAPER 4 Listening Part 1

02 You will hear people talking in eight different situations. For questions **1–8**, choose the best answer (**A**, **B** or **C**).

1 You overhear a woman talking about her car.
   How does she feel about it?

   A   She wants to get a bigger vehicle.
   B   She nearly always enjoys driving it.
   C   Her lifestyle makes her dependent on it.

2 You hear someone talking about a journey she made with a friend.
   How did they travel after they left the village?

   A   by bicycle
   B   by motorcycle
   C   by boat

3 You hear a man on the radio giving advice to listeners.
   What is he giving advice about?

   A   staying safe online
   B   playing online games
   C   buying things online

4 You overhear someone talking about a recent holiday.
   What disappointed her about the hotel where she stayed?

   A   Few meals were served.
   B   She did not like the room.
   C   The pool was not open.

5 You hear a woman talking about buying a work of art over the Internet.
   What does she say about it?

   A   The postage cost her rather a lot of money.
   B   She managed to buy a real bargain.
   C   It was less complicated than she had expected.

6 You hear a woman talking to her teenage son.
   What do they agree about?

   A   Computer games can be very enjoyable.
   B   Computer games can be good for the brain.
   C   Computer games can encourage bad behaviour.

7 You overhear a teenage girl talking about somebody arriving late.
   How does she feel now?

   A   sorry that she was unkind
   B   angry that she missed the film
   C   glad that she said what she felt

8 You overhear two people talking in the street.
   Where has the woman just come from?

   A   an internet café
   B   a police station
   C   a supermarket

Test 5 Listening Part 2

You will hear an interview with a woman called Hannah Romero who takes photographs of waterfalls. For questions **9–18**, complete the sentences.

Photographing waterfalls

Hannah took her first waterfall photos when she was [__9__] years old.

She used a camera belonging to her [__10__] to take the photos in the mountains.

She believes that [__11__] is the best time of year to photograph waterfalls.

She avoids photographing waterfalls in [__12__] weather.

She loves taking photos of water hitting [__13__] below.

In winter, the photographer should avoid treading on any [__14__] that may appear in a picture.

The photographer ought to remove [__15__] from the scene.

Hannah likes to take pictures from the [__16__] of smaller waterfalls.

The most important thing when taking pictures is the [__17__] of the photographer.

Hannah once took a photo of [__18__] in a waterfall.

Test 5 — Listening Part 3

🎧 04 You will hear five different people talking about shopping for food. For questions **19–23**, choose from the list (**A–F**) what each speaker says. Use the letters only once. There is one extra letter which you do not need to use.

A I always spend more than I intended to.

B I avoid going shopping when I'm hungry.

C I dislike going shopping with other people.

D I usually buy fruit and vegetables last.

E I only buy things if their prices are reduced.

F I hate waiting in a long queue to pay.

Speaker 1 — 19
Speaker 2 — 20
Speaker 3 — 21
Speaker 4 — 22
Speaker 5 — 23

Test 5 — Listening Part 4

05 You will hear an interview with Sophie Morrison, a translator. For questions **24–30**, choose the best answer (**A**, **B** or **C**).

24 Why did Sophie take up translating?
   A She had studied modern languages at university.
   B She sometimes used to do translations for friends.
   C She enjoyed reading texts in other languages.

25 At present, which subject is she specialising in as a translator?
   A medicine
   B law
   C business

26 Which, according to Sophie, are the most difficult things to translate?
   A cultural references
   B informal expressions
   C scientific and technical words

27 Where does Sophie get most of her work?
   A directly from official organisations
   B through translation agencies
   C from contacts in private companies

28 How does she feel about her daily working hours?
   A They are always too long.
   B They shouldn't include evenings.
   C They vary too much.

29 What does she say about money?
   A She earns less now than she used to.
   B She thinks she pays too much tax.
   C She seldom gets paid on time.

30 Sophie believes that in the future
   A translating will all be done by machines.
   B more languages will need to be translated.
   C translators will have to be better trained.

Test 5

PAPER 5 Speaking Parts 1 and 2

Part 1 — 3 minutes (5 minutes for groups of three)

Interlocutor First of all, we'd like to know something about you.

- Tell us a little about the people in your family.
- What are your earliest memories from when you were a child?
- What do you like most about your home? Why?
- How much time do you spend at home? (What do you do there?)
- Apart from your home town, where would you most like to live? Why?

Part 2 — 4 minutes (6 minutes for groups of three)

Interlocutor In this part of the test, I'm going to give each of you two photographs. I'd like you to talk about your photographs on your own for about a minute, and also to answer a short question about your partner's photographs.

(Candidate A), it's your turn first. Here are your photographs on page C18 of the Speaking appendix (Task 1). They show **people staying in different places.**

I'd like you to compare the photographs, and say **what you think the people are enjoying about their holiday.**

All right?

Candidate A
1 minute

Interlocutor Thank you.

(Candidate B), **where would you rather stay during your holidays?**

Candidate B
approximately 20 seconds

Interlocutor Thank you.

Now, *(Candidate B)*, here are your photographs on page C19 of the Speaking appendix (Task 2). They show **people doing things that can sometimes be dangerous.**

I'd like you to compare the photographs, and say **why you think it's important to be careful in these situations.**

All right?

Candidate B
1 minute

Interlocutor Thank you.

(Candidate A), **have you ever been on a motorbike?**

Candidate A
approximately 20 seconds

Interlocutor Thank you.

Test 5 — Speaking Parts 3 and 4

Part 3

3 minutes (4 minutes for groups of three)

Interlocutor Now, I'd like you to talk about something together for about three minutes.

Here are some pictures of people learning to do different things.

Show candidates pictures on pages C20–C21 of the Speaking appendix.

First, talk to each other about **how difficult it is to learn to do these things**. Then decide **which two are the most useful to learn**.

Part 4

4 minutes (5 minutes for groups of three)

Interlocutor *Select any of the following questions, as appropriate:*

- **When you were a child, what was the most difficult thing you had to learn to do? (Why was it difficult?)**
- **Do you think some people find it easier to learn new skills than others? (Why?/Why not?)**
- **What do you think is the best way to learn another language? (Why?)**

Thank you. That is the end of the test.

> *Select any of the following questions, as appropriate:*
> - **What do you think?**
> - **Do you agree?**
> - **And you?**

Test 6 PAPER 1 Reading Part 1

You are going to read an extract from a novel. For questions **1–8**, choose the answer (**A**, **B**, **C** or **D**) which you think fits best according to the text.

Mark your answers **on the separate answer sheet**.

Dick Sterling put the phone down. His hands were trembling. He was furious with himself for failing to persuade his boss in Delhi, Keith Lennox, to support him, and was disgusted at the mixture of veiled threats and vague promises Lennox had made. 'He knows too much' – the words still rang in his ears. He wondered, not for the last time, just what it was that Vish, the office manager of the factory, knew. How could it be so important that the company's position in India could be threatened by it? It simply didn't make sense. Dick glanced at his watch. Four o'clock. He called for his driver, Gopal. He'd had enough for the day.

Dick sat gloomily in the back of the car, going over in his mind the events which had led up to the present crisis. How had he got himself into this impossible situation? It should never have happened, yet somehow, looking back, it seemed inevitable. Perhaps he was beginning to believe in fate?

He had arrived three years earlier to take over as general manager of Trakton's factory in Madras. India was, of course, only one of the many countries in which Trakton operated. Dick had been transferred to Madras from Nigeria in fact, after a series of other overseas appointments. Each of the overseas factories had a general manager appointed from headquarters to oversee the management of the local workforce. In India this had worked particularly well. The Indian staff were highly trained and efficient. They were also generally easy to work with; the company's enlightened industrial relations policy had made sure of that. Salaries were higher than the average, there was a good pensions scheme and generous health insurance benefits. Trakton boasted that it had not lost a day in strikes for over fifteen years.

Dick had found his senior Indian colleagues particularly good to work with. They knew their jobs inside out and were clearly committed to the company. Many of them had been with Trakton for the whole of their working lives, starting in the factory and working their way up to become managers. They were a good team.

The only exceptions had been Visvanathan, or 'Vish' as he was known, the office manager, and his wife Molly. Molly was in charge of the Personnel Department. For reasons Dick had only gradually understood, Vish and Molly were regarded by the rest of the senior staff as somehow 'special'. They behaved as if they had special privileges and expected other staff to defer to them. Dick slowly realised that they controlled other staff members through a combination of threats and promises. Given their positions, they could make life very difficult for anyone who opposed them. Likewise, they could make life easy for those who did what they wanted.

Dick knew that this sort of behaviour happened to varying degrees in every culture and didn't think much of it. Indeed, in the first few weeks after his arrival, both Vish and Molly had been all smiles and helpfulness. They had invited Dick and his wife Sally to dinner too. Their newly built house was in the fashionable, up-and-coming Kalakshetra Colony, close to the sea. Dick had been suitably impressed by the expensively furnished house, which was full of the most modern household equipment. He had half-wondered, innocently, whether Vish had had to borrow money to pay for it all.

1   What was Dick's reaction to his conversation with Lennox?

    A   He regretted not telling Lennox what Vish knew.
    B   He did not want to stay at work any longer.
    C   He appeared calm but in fact was very angry.
    D   He was angry with his boss for breaking his promises.

2   When he was in his car, Dick thought that

    A   he could not have prevented the situation occurring.
    B   the situation was not as serious as it at first appeared.
    C   he could deal with the situation relatively easily.
    D   somebody else might help him handle the situation.

3   Before he took charge of the Madras factory,

    A   he had been working at Trakton's headquarters.
    B   he had spent three years doing another job in India.
    C   he had had a number of jobs in different countries.
    D   he had never worked for Trakton before.

4   What is meant by 'enlightened' in line 29?

    A   based on the aim of making maximum profit
    B   showing an understanding of people's needs
    C   given very little importance by the bosses
    D   costing the employers much less than it used to

5   A lot of the bosses at Trakton

    A   were keen to leave the firm.
    B   had not deserved promotion.
    C   had been manual workers.
    D   disliked each other intensely.

6   What does 'those' in line 51 refer to?

    A   other employees at the factory
    B   the office manager and his wife
    C   staff in the most senior positions
    D   Dick Sterling and Keith Lennox

7   How did Dick feel about the way Vish and Molly treated the other employees?

    A   He had never known anything similar before.
    B   He was extremely worried about its possible effects.
    C   He thought that this only happened in India.
    D   He realised this occurred throughout the world.

8   What does the writer suggest in the final paragraph?

    A   Both Dick and Vish lived in expensive houses.
    B   Vish was going to ask Dick to lend him some money.
    C   Dick should have realised that Vish was dishonest.
    D   Trakton paid Vish an extremely high salary.

Test 6 — Reading Part 2

You are going to read an article about a famous picture of the Earth taken by astronauts circling the moon. Seven sentences have been removed from the article. Choose from the sentences **A–H** the one which fits each gap (**9–15**). There is one extra sentence which you do not need to use.

The first picture of Earth from space
by Steve Connor

The first picture of our world taken from space was published over 40 years ago, yet it still has remarkable power.

They went to the moon, but ended up discovering the Earth. The crew of the US space vehicle Apollo 8 were the first people to leave Earth's orbit and they had been prepared for just about every possibility. The only exception was the astonishing sight of seeing our own planet above the horizon of the moon.

It later became known as 'Earthrise', from the word *sunrise*. This image of a small blue world rising in the dark vastness of space over the sun-lit surface of the moon was to become a constant reminder of just how alone, and how delicate, our planet really is. **9** Remarkably, it was taken over 40 years ago.

The three-man crew of Apollo 8 – Frank Borman, Jim Lovell and Bill Anders – were the first people to circle the moon. They flew around the far side, which is not visible from Earth. **10** They were not able to see or radio Earth for the duration of their journey behind the moon, and it was only when they had completed the orbit that they could again communicate with Mission Control Centre in Houston, Texas.

Perhaps surprisingly, for the first few orbits the crew had their backs to the Earth as it reappeared over the moon's horizon and did not see the now-famous view that would change their lives. **11** 'Look at that picture over there! Isn't that something?' he said, his words captured for history on the on-board tape recorder.

They quickly searched for a camera – the first couple of images of 'Earthrise' were in black and white, the following photos were taken in colour. It is these photographs, taken approximately 350,000 kilometres from Earth, that became the favourite images of the environmental movement.

12 It was a symbol of warmth and life in a bare desert of deathly coldness.

'Earthrise' would change forever our view of our own planet. It summed up the fragility of a place that seems so immense to the people who live there, but so tiny when viewed from the relatively short distance of its companion in space. Following the 1968 pictures, hundreds of still images were taken of Earth during the nine Apollo flights to the moon, but in 1972 manned flights to the moon ended. **13**

Astronomer Carl Sagan caught the mood well when another picture of Earth was taken from space, by the Voyager 1 spacecraft in 1990. **14** In this picture, the Earth appeared as a 'pale blue dot' surrounded by the vastness of space, like a tiny bit of dust caught in the sunshine.

'Look again at that dot,' he said a few years later. 'That's here. That's home. That's us. **15** Our imagined self-importance, the false belief that we have some special position in the universe, is challenged by this point of light. Our planet is a lonely little place in endless space.'

A Consequently, only 24 people have actually seen the whole of the Earth from space.

B On it everyone you love, everyone you know, everyone you ever heard of, every human being who ever was, lived out their lives.

C It was only on the fourth time round that one of the men turned and saw it.

D This time the distance was nearly six billion kilometres.

E Borman, however, has always claimed that he took it.

F It was a picture that would eventually lead to a thousand environmental movements, such was its effect on the public consciousness.

G They showed the clear contrast between the grey, empty surface of the lifeless moon and the bright blue-and-white ball of the fertile Earth.

H They were also in effect the first people to lose contact with their own planet.

Test 6 — Reading Part 3

You are going to read an article about people eating in unfamiliar restaurants. For questions **16–30**, choose from the people (**A–E**). The people may be chosen more than once. When more than one answer is required, these may be given in any order.

Mark your answers **on the separate answer sheet**.

Which person

was misunderstood by a member of the restaurant staff?	16	
particularly liked the variety of flavours?	17	
wishes they had not eaten part of the meal?	18	19
was impressed by the appearance of the staff?	20	
suddenly lost their appetite?	21	
sent back part of their meal?	22	
at first felt uncomfortable eating on their own?	23	
enjoyed a drink more than they had expected?	24	
ate there because there was nowhere else they could go?	25	
enjoyed eating home cooking?	26	
spent a lot more money than they had intended?	27	
says one part of the meal was too hot?	28	
didn't mind having to wait for a table?	29	
found the food to be much better than they had expected?	30	

A Martin Ryan

I'm from a small village and I'd never actually eaten in a fast-food restaurant before. The place looked clean and the employees were smartly dressed, and after I'd ordered and received my meal on a tray I paid the bill, which seemed quite reasonable. I can't say the burger and chips were particularly exciting, though, and they must have left the apple pie in the microwave too long because it burnt my tongue, but I was pleasantly surprised by the quality of the orange juice. I thought the background music was well chosen, and I liked the fact I wasn't the only person eating by myself.

B Asha Kumar

I was on a coach near Paris when we pulled into a motorway service station, and as we wouldn't be stopping again all day, I had no choice but to have a meal in the only restaurant there. It was self-service, though for hot food you had to ask someone to serve you across the counter. That was a problem, because when I asked for fish, in my terrible French, he thought I meant the chicken. Anyway, I eventually got my meal, and sat down at a table with a view of a lorry park. The food, I thought, would be equally dull, but that wasn't the case at all. Superbly cooked, and with first-rate ingredients, it had nothing in common with motorway food elsewhere. Though maybe I shouldn't have been surprised as this, after all, was France.

C Marco Foncseca

This was my first experience of Indian cooking and it certainly won't be my last. It was a small, welcoming restaurant where all the meals were made according to traditional recipes in the family kitchen that formed part of the house where they lived. The food was great, quite hot but certainly not too spicy, and what I liked most about it was the way everything had its own distinctive taste. It was so good that I ate an enormous amount, and really I should have stopped after I'd eaten the curry, but I couldn't resist having a huge dessert, too. That was a mistake because afterwards I felt a bit too full. Though any discomfort soon passed when I saw the bill, which was far lower than I'd expected.

D Hanif Badawi

The restaurant was recommended in the city guide, and although my friends and I had booked a table, when we arrived the head waiter apologised but said he couldn't seat us immediately. That actually suited me, as it gave me time to make a couple of phone calls, and when we eventually sat down, I felt quite relaxed. The soup was excellent, and when the waiters started bringing delicious-looking main courses for the others, I was really looking forward to mine. Until, that was, I saw what was on my plate. It didn't look properly cooked and I no longer felt hungry. I felt like sending it back but the waiters were very busy and I didn't want to put them to any trouble. Now I think I should have done, as I didn't enjoy it at all.

E Sophie McPherson

I was staying in a hotel and I thought I'd try the restaurant there. There was a queue, which was a little annoying, and when I sat down I was aware I was the only person at a table for one, and the thought that people were looking at me was making me nervous. Then I thought 'So what? I'm here to enjoy myself,' and I did! I ordered the best items on the menu, food I'd always wanted to try, and soon forgot about the other people eating there. I was running up a massive bill, which was exactly what I'd told myself I wouldn't do, but I didn't care. I insisted on having everything done just the way I liked it, asking the waitress to replace some vegetables that were overcooked and a drink that wasn't quite cool enough, but when I'd finished, I gave her one of the most generous tips she'd ever had.

Test 6 — PAPER 2 Writing Part 1

You **must** answer this question. Write your answer in **120–150** words in an appropriate style.

1. You applied to work at an international summer camp for children, and you have now received a reply from the manager, Martin Wilson. Read Mr Wilson's letter and the notes you have made. Then write a letter to Mr Wilson, using **all** your notes.

> *I am afraid the position you applied for is no longer available. We may, however, be able to offer you evening work.* — **No, because ...**
>
> *Alternatively, there is the possibility of full-time work at our camp in the mountains, although we are not yet sure whether we will need more staff there.* — **Ask when they'll know**
>
> *Please inform us whether you would be interested in either of these positions, and if so, indicate to us your preferred dates either in July or August.* — **Give details**
>
> *For any position with us it is of course essential that you have a good level of spoken English, and that you are able to get on well with people of all ages!* — **Definitely**
>
> *We look forward to hearing from you.*
>
> *Yours sincerely,*
>
> *M. Wilson*
> *Manager*

Write your **letter**. You must use grammatically correct sentences with accurate spelling and punctuation in a style appropriate for the situation.

Test 6 — Writing Part 2

Write an answer to **one** of the questions **2–5** in this part. Write your answer in **120–180** words in an appropriate style.

2   You see this announcement in the magazine of an English summer school.

> **Summer sports**
>
> The school intends to offer sporting activities outside lesson times, so we would like to know which sports our students would prefer. Football, basketball, tennis, swimming and cycling have been suggested. Write an article
> - telling us which two of these five sports you would like to play, and why
> - suggesting one other sport and saying why you think we should include it.

Write your **article**.

3   You have had a class discussion on the harmful effects of cars on people's lives and on the environment. Now your teacher has asked you to write a report on public transport in your town. You should include information on the services available, say whether they meet the needs of everyone in the town, and suggest how the transport system could be improved.

Write your **report**.

4   You have decided to enter an international short story competition. The competition rules say that the story must **begin** with the following words.

By the time they reached the top of the mountain, it was nearly dark and heavy snow was starting to fall.

Write your **story**.

5   Answer **one** of the following two questions based on **one** of the titles below. Write the letter **(a)** or **(b)** as well as the number **5** in the question box.

(a) [author/name of book]

Novels can have happy or sad endings, or leave what finally happens a mystery. Write an **essay** describing the ending of this book, and saying whether you think it is a good way of ending the story.

(b) [author/name of book]

A local film producer is thinking of making a film of the book you have read, and has asked you for more information. Write a **report** on the book for the producer, describing the main events and saying why the story would or would not be successful as a film.

Test 6

PAPER 3 Use of English Part 1

For questions **1–12**, read the text below and decide which answer (**A**, **B**, **C** or **D**) best fits each gap. There is an example at the beginning (**0**).

Mark your answers **on the separate answer sheet**.

Example:

0 **A** stands   **B** goes   **C** stays   **D** lies

0	A ▭ B ▭ C ▭ D ▬

St Lucia

The island of St Lucia, which **(0)** ..... between St Vincent and Martinique, is said to be one of the most attractive in the Caribbean. Measuring 44 kilometres long and 22 kilometres in width, it has a central mountain **(1)** ..... which runs the length of the island. There are white sandy beaches with wonderful **(2)** ..... of the two tall volcanoes called the Pitons, **(3)** ..... of which are covered – like most of the island – in dense forest.

The climate is hot and tropical **(4)** ..... the year, with average daily temperatures of about 27°C. Showers can occur in any month, although they are usually **(5)** ..... fairly quickly.

Not surprisingly, St Lucia is extremely **(6)** ..... with tourists. There is a wide range of **(7)** ..... , from camping to luxury hotels, and it is very well **(8)** ..... by sea and air with the rest of the world. **(9)** ..... this, the island remains largely unspoilt and there are many quiet places to visit.

Not far from the coastal areas there are beautiful waterfalls in spectacular green valleys, often with **(10)** ..... anybody else about. The roads are narrow and winding, so it is not **(11)** ..... to travel any distance by car. A much better way to **(12)** ..... to know the countryside of this lovely island is on horseback.

1	**A** queue	**B** range	**C** row	**D** series
2	**A** views	**B** scenes	**C** looks	**D** sights
3	**A** either	**B** all	**C** both	**D** each
4	**A** around	**B** while	**C** throughout	**D** over
5	**A** past	**B** over	**C** through	**D** beyond
6	**A** liked	**B** favourite	**C** enjoyed	**D** popular
7	**A** housing	**B** shelter	**C** sleeping	**D** accommodation
8	**A** connected	**B** joined	**C** related	**D** united
9	**A** Since	**B** Although	**C** Despite	**D** However
10	**A** nearly	**B** hardly	**C** almost	**D** just
11	**A** suitable	**B** favourable	**C** acceptable	**D** advisable
12	**A** want	**B** have	**C** get	**D** need

Test 6 — Use of English Part 2

For questions **13–24**, read the text below and think of the word which best fits each gap. Use only **one** word in each gap. There is an example at the beginning (**0**).

Write your answers **IN CAPITAL LETTERS on the separate answer sheet**.

Example: **0** ONE

The Northern Lights

Surely (0) ...*one*... of the most amazing sights on Earth is the display of natural light in the night sky known (13) .... the Northern Lights. It is something everyone should see (14) .... least once in their life.

These lights, (15) .... are mainly visible in the Arctic region, are caused when material from the sun reaches the Earth's magnetic field. On the (16) .... the most common colours are green and red, although sometimes blue or purple lights can be seen. They often look (17) .... brightly coloured clouds dancing across the sky, in displays that can last several hours.

(18) .... you want to observe the Northern Lights, it's best to get as close to the North Pole as possible during the winter, in (19) .... of the extreme cold. Seeing the lights in the short Arctic summer is not really possible in view of the (20) .... that they are only visible in darkness, and during the months (21) .... the sun never sets there is daylight 24 hours a day.

Weather conditions also (22) .... a big difference. The lights cannot be seen (23) .... the sky is clear, so there must be no fog or heavy clouds. Bright moonlight can also reduce the intensity of the lights and because of (24) .... you should avoid any nights that have a full moon.

Test 6 — Use of English Part 3

For questions **25–34**, read the text below. Use the word given in capitals at the end of some of the lines to form a word that fits in the gap **in the same line**. There is an example at the beginning (**0**).

Write your answers **IN CAPITAL LETTERS on the separate answer sheet**.

Example: **0** O P E R A T I O N

Sudden storm

A massive clean-up (0) *operation* is now under way in the south-west of	**OPERATE**
the country after a (25) .... storm unexpectedly struck the region.	**POWER**
Among the worst affected were (26) .... areas, where many small	**COAST**
boats were sunk or destroyed, though, (27) .... , there are no reports	**FORTUNE**
of anyone missing or seriously injured.	
In many towns, however, there was (28) .... damage to property,	**EXTENT**
with trees and fences blown over. In one street, almost every house	
had its roof blown off, leaving many families (29) .... until repairs	**HOME**
can be carried out. The (30) .... conditions also affected transport links	**WIND**
leading to the closure of motorways and the (31) .... of nearly all rail	**CANCEL**
services.	
Further inland, where the monthly average (32) .... is about 80mm,	**RAIN**
over 100mm fell in just a few hours. This resulted in several rivers	
bursting their banks and flooding huge areas of (33) .... land. Some	**AGRICULTURE**
villages were (34) .... cut off by the rapidly rising water, although	**TEMPORARY**
communications have now been restored in most places.	

Test 6 — Use of English Part 4

For questions **35–42**, complete the second sentence so that it has a similar meaning to the first sentence, using the word given. **Do not change the word given**. You must use between **two** and **five** words, including the word given. Here is an example (0).

0   You should continue to study every day.

   CARRY

   You should .... every day.

The gap can be filled by the words 'carry on studying', so you write:

Example: | 0 | CARRY ON STUDYING |

Write **only** the missing words **IN CAPITAL LETTERS on the separate answer sheet**.

---

35 Please don't leave the building because we might need to speak to you again.

   CASE

   Please don't leave the building .... to speak to you again.

36 'Don't be late again, Jamie,' said the teacher.

   TOLD

   The teacher .... late again.

37 A well-known director is making a film of Jennifer Shaw's latest novel.

   BEING

   A film of Jennifer Shaw's latest novel .... a well-known director.

38 We hadn't expected the weather to be so bad.

   WORSE

   The weather .... expected.

39 I had trouble printing documents from the computer.

   DIFFICULT

   I .... documents from the computer.

40 They don't let us use mobile phones in the library.

   ALLOWED

   In the library, ... use mobile phones.

41 Is that film likely to be shown on TV?

   CHANCE

   Is there .... being shown on TV?

42 I'm afraid we don't have any bread left.

   RUN

   I'm afraid .... bread.

Test 6 — PAPER 4 Listening Part 1

You will hear people talking in eight different situations. For questions **1–8**, choose the best answer (**A**, **B** or **C**).

1 You hear a man talking on the phone to a computer technician.
   Why has he called?

   A to make a complaint
   B to ask for some advice
   C to apologise for a mistake

2 You hear a teenager talking about the summer job he does.
   How does he usually feel when he is working?

   A bored
   B tired
   C relaxed

3 You overhear a young man talking to a friend.
   What does he regret?

   A not telling the truth
   B not spending enough
   C not staying at home

4 You hear two people talking.
   How does the man feel now?

   A very relieved
   B highly amused
   C quite worried

5 You switch on the radio during a programme.
   What is the programme about?

   A wildlife
   B history
   C farming

6 You turn on the radio and hear part of a play.
   Where is the scene taking place?

   A in a railway station
   B in the street
   C on a bus

7 You hear a teenager talking on the phone about where she lives now.
   What does she think of her new home?

   A It's like her previous house.
   B It's too far from her school.
   C It's difficult to get used to.

8 You overhear a young man talking about a job he had.
   Why did he leave work?

   A He wanted to travel.
   B He didn't like his job.
   C His boss sacked him.

Test 6 — Listening Part 2

You will hear part of a radio programme about reducing the amount of packaging used by supermarkets. For questions **9–18**, complete the sentences.

Supermarket packaging

Supermarkets are being forced to change their attitude to excessive packaging by [9] .

According to a study, around [10] of people want to reduce waste.

Some items in packages, such as [11] , are also wrapped individually.

Most people think it is wrong to wrap [12] in plastic.

Shoppers at some stores can now put excess packaging into [13] when they pay.

Some people suggest giving bad [14] to supermarkets that use too much packaging.

According to the manufacturers, a lot of packaging is [15] nowadays.

An official organisation thinks that supermarkets should pay a special [16] .

Some suggest that people should buy more in [17] instead of in supermarkets.

Shoppers rarely receive free [18] these days.

Test 6 — Listening Part 3

🎧 08 You will hear five different people talking about online activities. For questions **19–23**, choose from the list (**A–F**) what each speaker says. Use the letters only once. There is one extra letter which you do not need to use.

A You have to be careful not to spend too much money.

B You shouldn't give too much personal information.

C You can easily spend too much time doing this.

D You frequently receive interesting messages.

E You can work from home if you do this.

F You learn to see things from different points of view.

Speaker 1 — 19

Speaker 2 — 20

Speaker 3 — 21

Speaker 4 — 22

Speaker 5 — 23

Test 6 — Listening Part 4

09 You will hear a young woman called Joanna Riley giving a talk at a secondary school about her work looking after an area of countryside. For questions **24–30**, choose the best answer (**A**, **B** or **C**).

24 Joanna decided she wanted to do her present job when she was
  A a university student.
  B doing a different job.
  C still at secondary school.

25 Joanna's duties include
  A replacing wooden fences and gates.
  B protecting animals and trees.
  C repairing damaged footpaths.

26 What is special about Joanna's part of the countryside?
  A Lots of visitors go there.
  B The weather is extreme.
  C It is exceptionally large.

27 What is the most difficult part of her job?
  A putting fires out when the weather is hot and dry
  B sorting out problems between visitors and local people
  C preventing the illegal hunting of animals and birds

28 Joanna only feels depressed when she
  A sees rubbish left by visitors.
  B has to work in the dark in winter.
  C is alone for many hours.

29 What new power does Joanna now have?
  A She can temporarily close her area to visitors.
  B In extreme cases, she can arrest people.
  C She can make people pay for damage they cause.

30 Joanna says that anyone wanting to become a ranger should
  A apply for a job in their home area.
  B do voluntary work in the countryside.
  C first study geography at university.

Test 6 — PAPER 5 Speaking Parts 1 and 2

Part 1

3 minutes (5 minutes for groups of three)

Interlocutor First of all, we'd like to know something about you.

- Which school subject do/did you enjoy studying most? (Why?)
- Do you find it easy to study at home? (Why?/Why not?)
- Do you prefer studying with other people or on your own? (Why?)
- In what ways do you think English will be useful to you?
- Apart from English, which other language would you most like to learn? Why?

Part 2

4 minutes (6 minutes for groups of three)

Interlocutor In this part of the test, I'm going to give each of you two photographs. I'd like you to talk about your photographs on your own for about a minute, and also to answer a short question about your partner's photographs.

(Candidate A), it's your turn first. Here are your photographs on page C22 of the Speaking appendix (Task 1). They show **people at home in their free time**.

I'd like you to compare the photographs, and say **which you think is a better way to relax**.

All right?

Candidate A
1 minute

Interlocutor Thank you.

(Candidate B), **do you enjoy reading?**

Candidate B
approximately 20 seconds

Interlocutor Thank you.

Now, *(Candidate B)*, here are your photographs on page C23 of the Speaking appendix (Task 2).

They show **people going to work.**

I'd like you to compare the photographs, and say **what is uncomfortable about travelling in these conditions.**

All right?

Candidate B
1 minute

Interlocutor Thank you.

(Candidate A), **do you ever ride a bicycle?**

Candidate A
approximately 20 seconds

Interlocutor Thank you.

Test 6 — Speaking Parts 3 and 4

Part 3

3 minutes (4 minutes for groups of three)

Interlocutor

Now, I'd like you to talk about something together for about three minutes.

I'd like you to imagine that a website is organising a competition called 'Unusual Holiday Photographs'. Here are some photographs that people have sent in for the competition.

Show candidates pictures on page C24 of the Speaking appendix.

First, talk to each other about **why the people might have taken these photographs on their holidays**. Then decide **which photograph should win the competition**.

Part 4

4 minutes (5 minutes for groups of three)

Interlocutor

Select any of the following questions, as appropriate:

- Why do you think some tourists take so many photos?
- What should you do if you want to take a good photo of friends or family?
- What's the most interesting photo you've ever seen?

Thank you. That is the end of the test.

> *Select any of the following questions, as appropriate:*
> - What do you think?
> - Do you agree?
> - And you?

Sample answer sheet: Paper 1

184 | Sample answer sheets

Paper 1

Sample answer sheet: Paper 3

Sample answer sheet: Paper 3

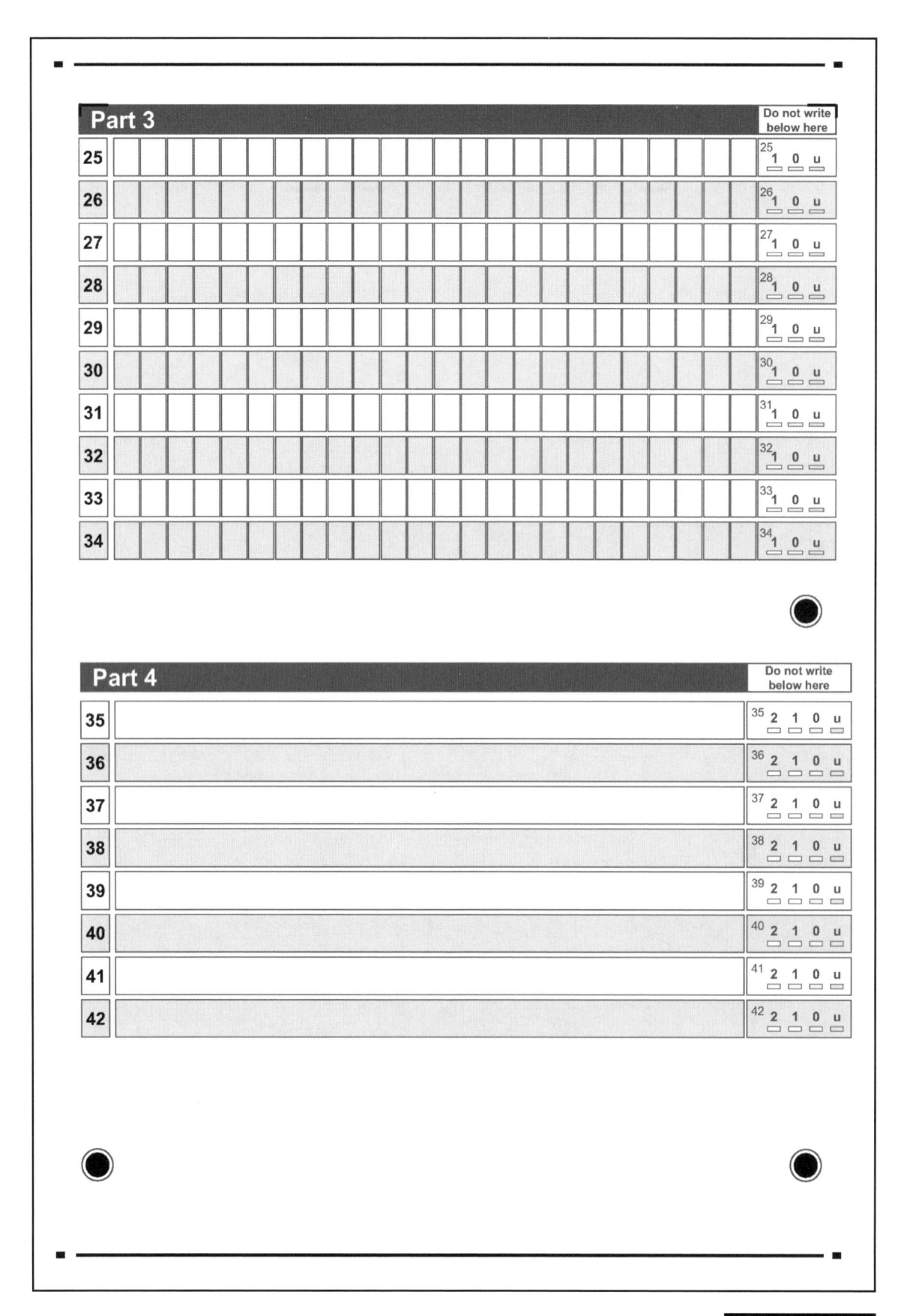

Sample answer sheet: Paper 4

UNIVERSITY of CAMBRIDGE
ESOL Examinations

SAMPLE

Candidate Name
If not already printed, write name in CAPITALS and complete the Candidate No. grid (in pencil).

Candidate Signature

Examination Title

Centre

Supervisor:
If the candidate is ABSENT or has WITHDRAWN shade here

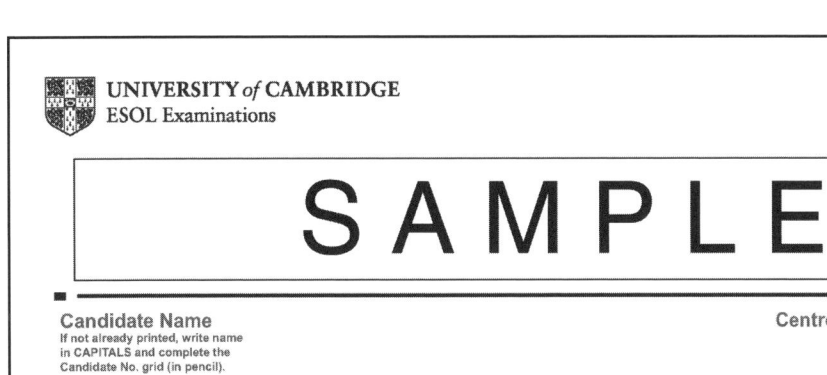

Centre No.

Candidate No.

Examination Details

Test version: A B C D E F J K L M N   Special arrangements: S H

Candidate Answer Sheet

Instructions

Use a PENCIL (B or HB).
Rub out any answer you wish to change using an eraser.

Parts 1, 3 and **4:**
Mark ONE letter for each question.

For example, if you think **B** is the right answer to the question, mark your answer sheet like this:

Part 2:
Write your answer clearly in CAPITAL LETTERS.

Write one letter or number in each box.
If the answer has more than one word, leave one box empty between words.

For example:

Turn this sheet over to start.

REPRODUCED WITH THE PERMISSION OF CAMBRIDGE ESOL

Photocopiable

Sample answer sheet: Paper 4

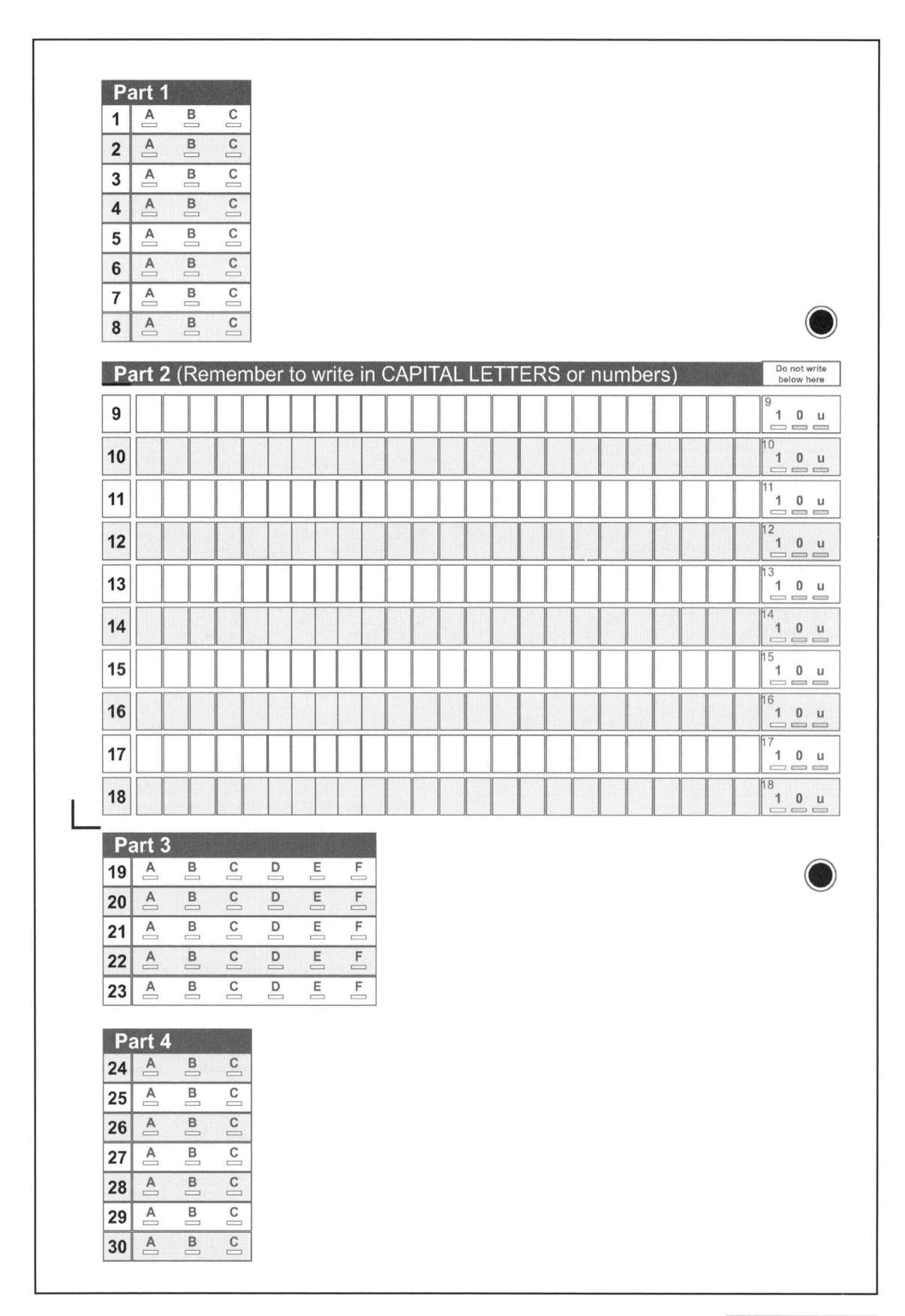

Acknowledgements

The author and publishers are grateful to the following for reviewing the material: Christine Barton; Anthea Bazin; Hayden Berry; Petrina Cliff; Caroline Cooke; Rosie Ganne; David Jay; Nick Shaw.

Development of this publication has made use of the Cambridge International Corpus (CIC). The CIC is a computerised database of contemporary spoken and written English which currently stands at over one billion words. It includes British English, American English and other varieties of English. It also includes the Cambridge Learner Corpus, developed in collaboration with the University of Cambridge ESOL Examinations. Cambridge University Press has built up the CIC to provide evidence about language use that helps to produce better language teaching materials.

The authors and publishers acknowledge the following sources of copyright material and are grateful for the permissions granted. While every effort has been made, it has not always been possible to identify the sources of all the material used, or to trace all copyright holders. If any omissions are brought to our notice, we will be happy to include the appropriate acknowledgements on reprinting.

NI Syndication for the adapted article on p. 12 'Alone to the North Pole' from 'Alone to the North Pole, Don't forget the Bikini' by Emma Smith, *Sunday Times* 8.2.09. Copyright © the Times and NI Syndication.com; Daily Telegraph for the adapted text on p. 16 'The benefits of online fitness training' from 'The benefits of web workouts' by Lucy Atkins, *Daily Telegraph* 1.6.09. Copyright © Telegraph Media Group Limited 2009; Cambridge University Press for the text on p. 67 from *In the Shadow of the Mountain Level 5*, by Helen Naylor. Copyright © Cambridge University Press 1999 and for the text and front cover on p. 165 from *He Knows too Much, Level 6*, by Alan Maley. Copyright © Cambridge University Press 1999. Reproduced with permission of Cambridge University Press; The Independent for the adapted text on p. 70 'I was getting out of training crying. Your mind plays tricks' by Richard Wilson, *The Independent* 7.6.09, for the adapted text on p. 110 'Getting rid of plastic bags' from 'The Big Question' by Michael McCarthy, *The Independent* 26.2.09 and for the adapted text on p. 167 'The first picture of earth from space' from 'Forty years since the first picture of earth from space' by Steve Connor, *The Independent* 10.1.09. Copyright © Independent Newspapers; Cambridge ESOL for the text on p. 74 from *Cambridge ESOL Handbook for Teachers FCE* (pre 2008 exam) and for the sample answer sheets at the back of the book. Reproduced by permission of Cambridge ESOL; Nick Inman for the adapted text on p. 108 'Writing Guidebooks' from 'Writers of Passage' *The Author* Spring 2008. www.nickinman.com; The Linguist for the adapted text on p. 127 'A year in China' from 'Bringing down the Great Wall' by Hannes Ortner, *The Linguist* April/May 2006 and for the adapted text on p. 129 'Get Blogging!' from 'Blog Standard' by Susan Purcell, *The Linguist* February/March 2009. Reproduced by permission of the Linguist (www.iol.org.uk); David Higham Associates and Random House for the text on p. 146 from *Blue Shoes and Happiness* by Alexander McCall Smith. Copyright © 2006. Published by Little Brown Book Group. Used by permission of Pantheon Books, a division of Random House Inc, Knopf Canada and David Higham Associates on behalf of the author; ArticleCity.com for the text on p. 148 'Skating on the Rideau Canal' from 'Hello From Ottawa' by Susanne Pacher. Copyright © 2001-Present ArticleCity.com.

For permission to reproduce photographs:
Mark Bourdillon p. 12; Bach Bach/Photolibrary.uk.com p. 14; WP Simon/Digital Vision/Getty Images p. 16; Visual Impact/Alamy p. 19; Ray Tang/Photolibrary.uk.com p. 70; Erik Isakson/Tetra Images/Imagestate p. 97; Photos India/Photolibrary.uk.com p. 108; simo-images/Alamy p. 110; TAO Images Limited/Photolibrary.uk.com p. 127; Corbis p. 129; HBO/Everett/Rex Features p. 146; Garry Black/Photolibrary.uk.com p. 148; Alan Maley (Cambridge University Press 1999, reproduced with permission) He Knows Too Much Level 6, p. 165; NASA Langley Research Center p. 167; Andres Rodriguez/Alamy (top), Julian Finney/Getty Images (bottom) p. C1; Golden Pixels LLC/Alamy (top), Maica/iStockphoto.com (bottom) p. C2; Koji Aoki/Photolibrary.uk.com (top), Daniel Berehulak/Getty Images (bottom) p. C3; Niall Benvie/Corbis (top), David Madison/Photolibrary.uk.com (bottom) p. C4; Jerónimo Alba/age fotostock/Imagestate (top), RubberBall/Alamy (bottom) p. C8; Jetta Productions/Lifesize/Getty Images (top), Ulrich Niehoff/Photolibrary.uk.com (bottom) p. C9; Imagesource/Photolibrary.uk.com (top, bottom) p. C12; Michael Hitoshi/Photodisc/Getty Images (top), Andrew Watson/Photolibrary.uk.com (bottom) p. C13; Picture Partners/Alamy (top), Andry A/Alamsyah/Alamy (bottom) p. C15; Hoberman Collection/Photolibrary.uk.com (top), Franck Dunouau/Photononstop/Photolibrary.uk.com (bottom) p. C16; Robert Daly/Photolibrary.uk.com (top), Daniel Dempster Photography/Alamy (bottom) p. C18; Justin Kase zsixz/Alamy (left), Purestock/Alamy (right) p. C19; Keith Morris/Alamy (top), Paul Baldesare/Alamy (bottom) p. C22; Dimitri Vervitsiotis/Photonica/Getty Images (top), Toby Burrows/Photolibrary.uk.com (bottom) p. C23; nobleIMAGES/Alamy (top left), Lewis Phillips/Photolibrary.uk.com (middle left), Carol Barrington/Alamy (top middle), Aurora Photos/Alamy (top right), Andrew Kemp/Alamy (bottom right), Christopher Pillitz/Alamy (middle right), Andy Sewell/Photolibrary.uk.com (bottom left), Radius Images/Alamy (middle) p. C24.
Illustrations: John Batten: pp. 10, 52, 54, 56, 95, 100, 114, 133, 152, 171
Janos Jantner: pp. 49, 72, C5, C6, C7, C10, C11, C14, C17, C20, C21

Audio recordings by John Green TEFL Audio. Engineer: Adam Helal; Editor: Tim Woolf; Producer: John Green. Recorded at ID Audio Studios, London.

Designed and typeset by eMC Design Ltd

Notes

Notes

Notes

Test 1 Training — Speaking Part 2

Task 1

A

B

Speaking appendix | Test 1 Speaking Part 2 | C1

Test 1 Training — Speaking Part 2

Task 2

> Why are the two different kinds of relationship important to teenagers?

A

B

Test 1 Exam practice — Speaking Part 2

What could be exciting about doing these things?

A

B

Test 1 Exam practice — Speaking Part 2

Why is the activity important to the different people?

A

B

Test 1 Training   Speaking Part 3

How useful are these things to the family? Which two things are most important to you?

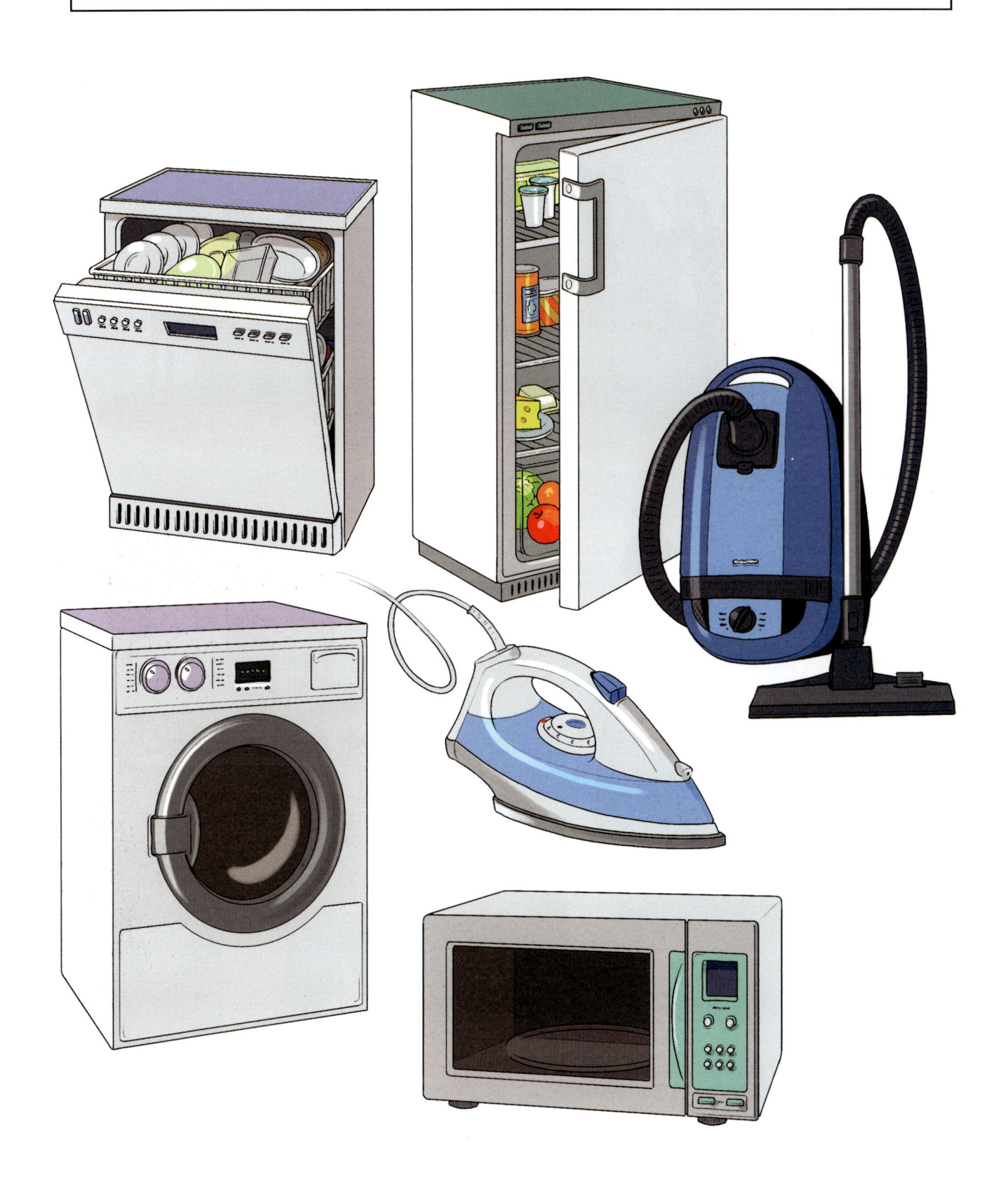

Speaking appendix   Test 1 Speaking Part 3 | C5

Test 1 Exam practice — Speaking Part 3

Which kinds of music would be popular with people in general?
Which two kinds would young people enjoy most?

Speaking appendix

Test 1 Speaking Part 3 | C7

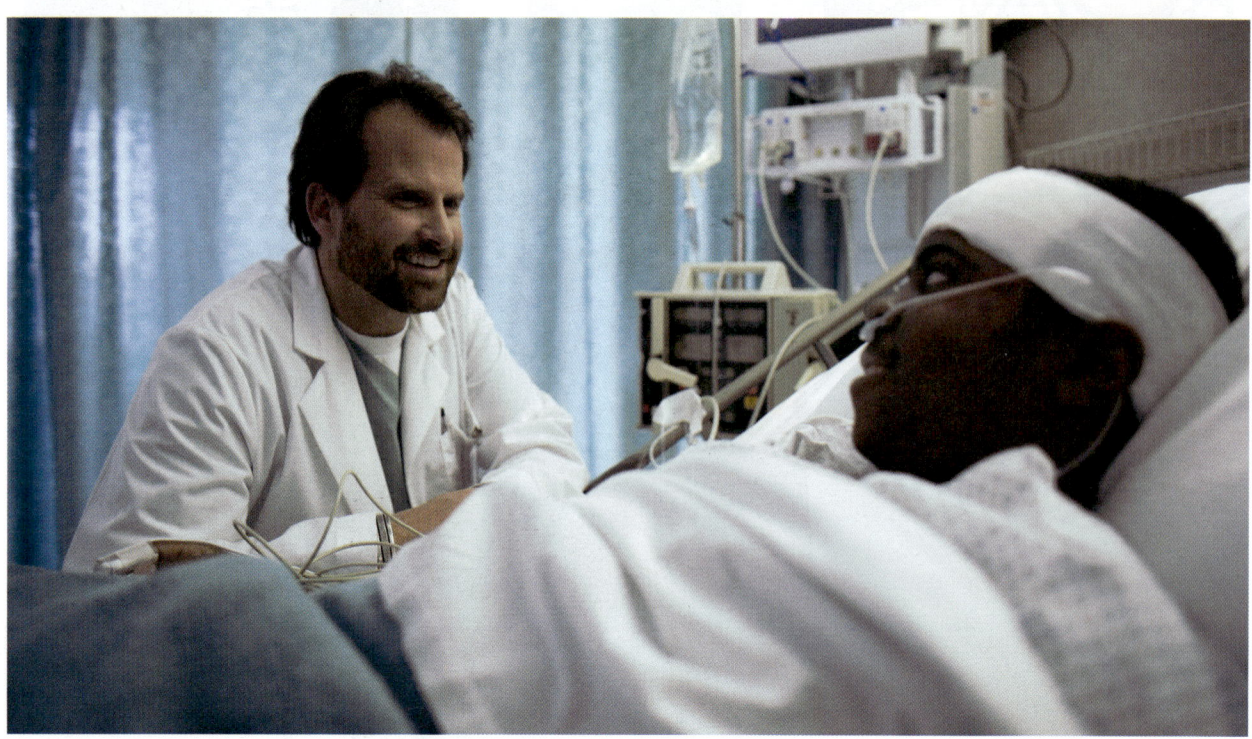

Test 2 Exam practice — Speaking Part 2

What do they probably like about their jobs?

A

B

Test 2 Exam practice — Speaking Part 2

What are the advantages of each way of communicating?

C

D

Test 2 Exam practice — Speaking Part 3

> What are the attractions of these kinds of places? Which two do you think would be the most interesting for a group of young people to visit?

Speaking appendix   Test 2 Speaking Part 3 | C11

Test 3 — Speaking Part 2

Task 1

> Why do you think people enjoy watching these kinds of programme?

Test 3 Speaking Part 2

Task 2

Why do people buy clothes in places like these?

Test 3 — Speaking Part 3

- How well could each of these ideas help people pass the time on a long journey?
- Which two would be the most enjoyable?

Test 4 Speaking Part 2

Task 1

> Why do people choose to listen to music in these different ways?

Test 4 Speaking Part 2

Task 2

Which way of life is better for the animals?

Test 4 — Speaking Part 3

- How useful is each of these places?
- Which would be the best one to live near?

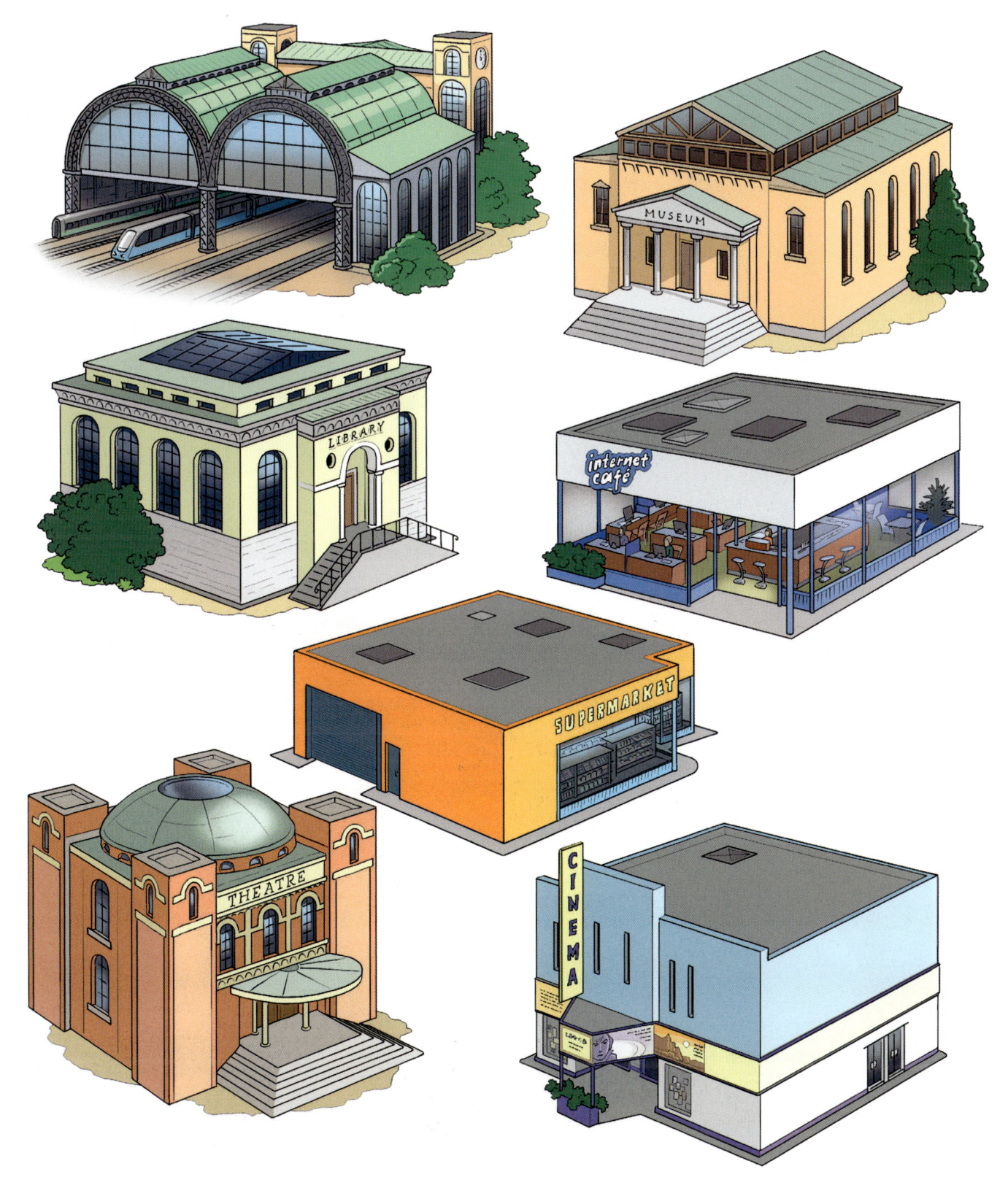

Test 5 Speaking Part 2

Task 1

> What do you think the people are enjoying about their holiday?

Test 5

Speaking Part 2

Task 2

> Why is it important to be careful in these situations?

Test 5

Speaking Part 3

- How difficult is it to learn to do these things?
- Which two are the most useful to learn?

Speaking appendix

Test 5 Speaking Part 3 | C21

Test 6

Speaking Part 2

Task 1

Which is a better way to relax?

Test 6

Speaking Part 2

Task 2

What is uncomfortable about travelling in these conditions?

Test 6 Speaking Part 3

- Why might people have taken these photographs on their holidays?
- Which photograph should win the competition?